MW00588462

## Praise for

## Building a Legacy of Love:
## Thriving in the Sandwich Generation

*"More often than not, the Sandwich Generation shift is usually an unexpected lifestyle occurrence that directly impacts family finances with no advance planning. The sudden transition can be very stressful and having immediate access to adequate and accurate information will minimize stress and assist with managing your new normal. Not only is the book filled with credible research, it is also a great reference guide for legal documents and financial guidance. Christy's book is the roadmap for anyone navigating this journey and definitely a must read if you have primary responsibility for an aging parent."*
**Carol Hunter, *The Money Mender***

*"Christy Yates' "Building A Legacy of Love: Inside the Sandwich Generation" book opened my eyes to a generation that I wasn't even aware of and I believe everyone should know about. Christy is an expert who guides us through the challenges and gifts with practical and heartfelt information, tools, and resources that are invaluable."*
**Kelly Mobeck, CPC, CEF Founder of Kelly J Mobeck Coaching**

*"I love the way Christy Yates takes us on her personal journey as a daughter and a caregiver. She brings me to tears in her transparency about the difficult decisions and the need to choose between our parents and our children. In this timely interdisciplinary look at the life of a generation, Christy Yates advances a new and powerful paradigm. Building a Legacy of Love is a must read for everyone to understand the phenomena of the Sandwich Generation."*
**Renee Balcom, founder & CEO Silver Lining Network**

# Building a
# Legacy of Love

## THRIVING IN THE SANDWICH GENERATION

CHRISTY BYRNE YATES, M.S.

ISBN: 978-1-7365457-0-6 (Paperback)
ISBN: 978-1-7365457-1-3 (E-Book)

Library of Congress Control Number: 2021905430

Cover and interior design Andy Meaden meadencreative.com

First printing edition 2021.

Yates Empowerment Strategies, LLC
7909 Walerga Rd. Suite 112
Sacramento, CA 95843


www.christyyates.com

# Dedication

To my children, may you embrace the legacy of love from all of us who have loved you, and may you continue that legacy on into the future.

For all those who are caregivers, may you recognize and embrace your immeasurable gift to the world.

# CONTENTS

# PREFACE

# SUNSETS

*Sunsets are proof that no matter what happens, every
day can end beautifully.*

**Kristen Butler**

I love Sunsets. I collect pictures of sunsets.

Sunrises are gorgeous, of course, but I'm not really an early riser, so I often miss them. In the fall of 2018, my husband and I were in Australia. We talked about getting up early and catching the Pacific Ocean sunrise, because we'd enjoyed so many Pacific Ocean sunsets as Californians. We set our alarm on a couple of occasions, but we never made it out the door to the beach. Sad, but there it is.

But I am a sunset lover.

I love how sunsets pick up the colors of the day and each one looks different. Sometimes after a cloudy afternoon, the sunset is harder to see, but it usually reflects what the day has been like. Ironically, some of the most colorful sunsets are vibrant *because* of smog or smoke or tumultuous weather.

Sunsets are also fleeting. To capture the true moment of sunset, we must focus on the horizon. It happens in a flash. It often is a flash.

We look to the west and watch the horizon. Clouds may impede the view, but if we watch closely, we can see the final waning moments of the sun. Then, not quite full dark. We detect a lingering glow, like staring at an LED bulb and then turning it off, and still our eyes see the glow. It's as if the room soaked up enough light to see us safely out the door.

So, too, the horizon keeps the radiance of the sun for a few moments so we can adjust our eyes and safely orient ourselves to movement, or curl up in a sleeping bag, or cuddle closer to a loved one, or transition to our next place.

Science explains the colors of the sunrise and sunset and the glow that hovers afterwards. It has to do with the spectrum of light, the gases present in the atmosphere, and a host of other variables; but beyond science, sunrises and sunsets have endless possibilities for the meaning of life. The terms for the post-sunset light are also fertile ground for metaphor: Afterglow. Blue Hour. Dusk. Twilight.

Many a poem has been dedicated to this topic, but for the purposes of this book, let's consider that we all experience the full spectrum of a day from sunrise to sunset, however long that day may be. Everyone's day is different, and even two people who are together throughout the day have two distinctly different experiences. Still, there is a sunset. And the sun will rise the next day.

A sunset can set the mood for the end of the day or reflect the mood of the day, depending on how we choose to see it.

Our choice makes all the difference.

We face many decisions in life and many changes and transitions— like sunrise to sunset. I've heard it said, "Nothing endures but change." With changes come choices, especially for parents. If our children embody the sunrise, full of possibility and excitement, our parents embody the sunset. We're wedged in between. We are the bit in the middle of the sandwich who must respond to continuing transitions and make difficult choices.

# My Story

*Mom wakes again, after nearly 30 minutes of sleep. She is groggy. She scowls, and looks at me, almost with a look of annoyance. "Where am I?" she asks.*

*"Mom, you're in the hospital," I tell her as gently as I can manage after answering the question multiple times.*

*"What? Why am I in the hospital?"*

*I tell her she has been having trouble breathing and that's why she has the oxygen tube in her nose. She's cranky. She jerks her head from side to side and scratches her head. "Where's Charlie?"*

*There it is. Where is Charlie? The love of her life. My dad—who died not three weeks ago. She doesn't remember. I've already had to tell her too many times. How do I keep breaking her heart? Am I doing the right thing in telling her? I've asked myself that too many times, as well.*

*"Mom..." She can tell by my voice, I think, because she looks at me with sad eyes. "He's dead?" She asks in a whisper. "He's dead," she says again with knowing despair. She weeps silently; hangs her head. Alzheimer's has muddled her memories and ability to hold onto much.*

*We are in the hospital because she has pleural effusion. Fluid has built up in the space between the lung tissue and the chest cavity. It functions a lot like pneumonia, and had that been the case, it would have been easier. That could have been solved, cured. She is easily out of breath. She can't do those things she loves the most—take a nice walk or go to church with my family.*

*The day before, I had arrived at her home to take her to church with my family. Her home is a lovely place that provides assisted living support, memory care, and some nursing. She sat with an on-duty nurse in the small office just off the community area. My mother wasn't up to going to church. Her hands gripped the chair for support, a quiet look on her face; she barely smiled, as if even that natural gesture were too much effort. She was pale, and the dark circles under her eyes weighed down her whole face. The nurses were concerned; she was far more lethargic than before. They pulled me aside to say she should go to the emergency room.*

*It took hours in the ER to learn that the cause of her fatigue and difficulty getting a breath was pleural effusion. They decided to admit her so that the next morning she could undergo a procedure to drain the fluid by inserting a needle into the pleural area. Lab tests would tell the cause of the build-up of fluid. They would lightly sedate her. It shouldn't hurt, but she would have to be still. I didn't know if she could do it, given her Alzheimer's and grief state.*

*After we complete the admissions process, I take her to her hospital room. The nurses ask me if I will stay with her. I hadn't thought of that. Why didn't I think of that, I ask myself, crushed with guilt. Naturally, given her confusion, she will orient to me more readily than changing shifts of nurses, no matter how compassionate they are. I have my husband bring me a change of clothing and my computer. I email my work that I will be out again and that I don't know how long. Then the panic sets in.*

*It is early Monday morning, and we are supposed to fly out on Wednesday. My oldest child, my son, is off to college, and I desperately want to go—I feel I have to. But my mother might still be in the hospital, confused, frightened, anxious, grieving. This is the dilemma I have most feared. The one I have successfully avoided for ten years.*

Choices like these are the heart of the struggle of the Sandwich Generation: the squeeze between parent and child—YOUR parent and YOUR child.

# The Sandwich Generation

Dorothy Miller, a social worker, coined the term "Sandwich Generation" in 1981 to describe women in their 30s and 40s who are "sandwiched" between raising children and caring for aging parents. A lot has changed since then. Primarily, the number of people who now find themselves in that demographic has increased dramatically. The age of people "sandwiched" has also risen. According to a Pew Research Study (one of a growing number of studies on this population), nearly 47% of Americans will find themselves in this situation. That's due to more women delaying childbirth past their 20s and the aging of the Baby Boomer Generation, one of the largest generation groups. Additionally, according to a 2019 "Parents, Kids & Money Survey," conducted by T. Rowe Price, an asset management company, more than a third of parents raising children between ages 8 and 14 are caring for an aging family member, and 68% of those folks had their aging family member living with them. A third of those families contribute up to $3,000 each month to the care of the aging parent.

Baby Boomers were born following World War II between 1946 and 1964. According to information gleaned from Center for Disease Control (CDC) National Vital Statistics Reports (NVSS), prior to 1946 birth rates in America were typically under three million per year. Between 1928 and 1946, there were about 47 million new births. After 1946, the birth rate jumped dramatically to an all-time high of around 4.3 million per year from 1957 to 1964. In all, the Baby Boomer Generation produced an estimated 76 million people. In 2011, the first of the baby Boomers turned 65. The rate of Baby Boomers reaching retirement age has increased at the same pace that the generation itself has grown. Those folks born at the tail end of the Baby Boomer Generation (1964) will reach 65 in 2029.

Couple those statistics with increased rates of longevity, and that's a lot of aging parents. According to the most recent data from the

Centers for Disease Control (CDC), in 2017 life expectancy in the U.S. is about age 78.6. While the average age of retirement varies by state, the overall average in the U.S. is age 63, with full Medicare benefits beginning at age 65. So, a large number of people are retiring and living another 12 years or more, and many of those do not have enough money or resources to live the life they were accustomed to, given that inflation rates hover around 2% overall, with peaks and dips here and there.

For many folks, retirement is a wonderful time of rejuvenation, relaxation, and even renewal. We conjure pictures of seniors on the golf course or cruising the Bahamas or playing bingo. But many seniors live on fixed incomes that barely provide for basic necessities. In 2018, the Kaiser Family Foundation (KFF) reported that in 2017 more than 14% of Americans over age 65 live below the poverty level. Seniors are faced with food insecurity and housing insecurity. This group of Americans is often plagued by inadequate health insurance or limited access to health care as well, which is a big reason so many families jump in to help, financially and otherwise.

More recently, as it relates to how the 2020 COVID-19 Pandemic impacted seniors, another KFF study found that as of 2018, about 6% of people over the age of 65 lived in a household with school-aged children. In addition, a related study from KFF found that while nearly half of those seniors living with school-aged children were white, COVID-19 disproportionately impacted people—and seniors—of color.

Several studies point to the ill effects of added stress facing people who are raising their own families as well as caring for an aging parent. A 2015 American Psychological Association study, "Stress in America: Paying with Our Health," suggested that women reported increased levels of stress as opposed to men. The most stress reportedly came from money concerns and family responsibilities. A 2019 update to the American Association of Retired Persons (AARP) Public Policy Institute report "Valuing the Invaluable" suggested that nearly 60% of family caregivers also work full time, which adds to stress levels. Also well documented is the association between stress and other diseases and ailments. There is a good reason why mindfulness practices and stress reduction techniques have become a burgeoning industry worldwide. And according to a study from the CDC's National Center for Health Statistics (NCHS), the use of anti-depressants and anti-anxiety medication increased by 65% between the years 1999 and 2014, and for the decade 2009-2010 to 2017-2018 anti-depressant use among adult women increased from 13.8% to 18.6%. Life in this squeeze is demanding and, consequently, stressful.

There is hope. While the majority of studies point to the negative impact of emotional and physical health that affects caregivers, a 2013 study published in the American Journal of Epidemiology suggested that some caregivers live longer than non-caregivers. Apparently, there may be health benefits from caregiving that are related to increases in stress-fighting hormones released during acts of compassion and support. People in the Sandwich Generation also report feeling happy about being able to aid an aging parent in their last years.

## Who This Book is For

You may already identify as someone in the **Sandwich Generation**. If so, I hope this book will provide some comfort as well as practical strategies to assist in the journey.

If you are **not quite there yet**—your parent is not retired but heading in that direction—or you don't have a family of your own, then this book can be a "heads up" about how to prepare yourself now to care for an aging parent while raising your own family. If your parent is not retiring soon or needing your care, this book can be food for thought about how to begin putting your own affairs in order. It's never too early, and your children will thank you for it!

If you are a **Baby Boomer** and an aging parent, this book offers practical ideas for you, also. What can you do to prepare yourself and your family for the future?

Let me be clear: I do not have all the answers for all situations. I have the perspective of a white, middle-class, working mother in a dual-income family. I acknowledge that this is only one segment of all the many families in our country or the world, and I've had lots of privilege in my life. I don't speak for everyone, and I don't claim to have all the answers for everyone. There is no one right way. There are disparities in healthcare, income, educational opportunities, and professional opportunities in the United States that make caring for children and elders significantly more difficult and costly for some. Systemic racism pervades all areas of our society and harshly impacts healthcare, education, childcare, and eldercare, so the struggle for people of color is increased and compromised. I care deeply about these issues, but this book will not adequately address those. I hope this book will still serve anyone faced with the tough choices between children and parents. The common thread, no matter your life circumstance, is that we all will lose people we love. Our elders generally pass first, so perhaps the best way to love our families is to prepare early.

## Back to Sunsets

Everyone's family is different. Who we call family is different. The make-up of family is different.

Many adults will care for an aging parent. The primary struggle for those in the Sandwich Generation, the key element that creates some added stress, is simultaneously having a family of one's own to raise and care for. There are folks who have small children and those who have young adults that are either still in the home or have returned home. There are those who not only have children in their home, but grandchildren as well, or children with special needs who will continue to need care throughout their adult life.

The tough part of being in the Sandwich Generation is being the primary adult providing support and sustenance for both or all. This is the real squeeze—and this book is an endeavor to ease the squeeze.

# 1

# STARTING A CONVERSATION

*Clouds come floating into my life, no longer to carry
rain or usher storm, but to add colour to my sunset sky.*

### Rabindranath Tagore

Both my parents died during the summer of 2015, seven weeks apart.
As I look back, it feels like it happened in a moment; but at the time,
it felt like eons.

How did I get the job as caretaker? I lived the closest. My parents
lived nearby in Sacramento; my brother was in Michigan; my sister,
initially down the road in the Bay Area, had moved to Montana.
Because I was nearby, my husband and I jumped in from time to
time to help my folks out with things—mostly computer stuff. My
parents had done a lot for us, as well. They hosted family gatherings,
offered sage advice when asked, and of course, free babysitting! But as
they aged, little by little, we began doing more and more. We helped
with some of the heavy lifting, literally, and continued as computer
and tech support, hooking up a new flat screen TV, providing endless
tutorials on how to use a VCR, then a DVD player, voicemail, and
eventually an introduction to the digital age and the use of cellphones
and automatic bill pay.

It almost seems synchronistic. Possibly meant to be.

I was the middle child, and like many middle children, I was a bit of a standout. Some of this was due to temperament, but mostly I stood out because at the age of six I was diagnosed with a serious illness: Juvenile Rheumatoid Arthritis (JRA). My disease was both chronic and acute. For much of my early years I was on bed rest and in a wheelchair. There were hospital stays, doctor visits, and lots of extra parental efforts to accomplish simple things. I remember my dad carrying me as a 10-year-old up to communion at our church.

Caring for my parents meant I could now give back the nurturing and support they gave me, as if our time together was coming full circle. I never felt like I "owed" them, but I was happy to jump in and offer help, like matching bookends.

In addition, I had spent most of my adult professional life as a case manager or casework supervisor for people with disabilities of one kind or another. I earned a master's in counseling psychology and eventually earned a credential as a school psychologist. I knew my way around assessment, developing interventions, setting goals, and structuring a plan to meet them.

My education and training as a school psychologist was extremely relevant. School psychologists differ from other psychologists in a number of ways. Not only are school psychologists trained in counseling—which is what many people think is a primary function—but they are well trained in human development, behavioral analysis, and how people learn, including psychological processing skills like visual processing, auditory processing, visual motor integration, memory, and attention. School psychologists are skilled assessors and are trained to use neuropsychological measures, cognitive measures, and social emotional measures. They are keen observers of people, especially those with a variety of disabilities. School psychologists do not diagnose mental health disorders using the Diagnostic and Statistical Manual, Fifth Edition (DSM V), which is used by clinical psychologists, psychiatrists, and other medical doctors. But they are skilled in differential diagnosis, since they are called upon to determine if a student meets criteria under the Federal Individuals with Disabilities Education Act (IDEA). Good school psychologists gather data from a variety of sources, observations, and instruments and don't simply rely on numbers from an IQ test. In addition, they are well versed in how certain disabilities manifest in real life—what they look like, how they show up, and what impact they have on learning and functioning. Then, with all of that information, they help design interventions, accommodations, and supports, and they monitor progress.

School psychologists also tend to be constantly learning themselves. I geek out when I see a new workshop on something related to learning, psychosocial development, disabilities, or neuroscience.

When I first noticed we needed to do more caretaking with my parents, I took a gerontology course at a local community college. It was a course in policy and services, sort of a big-picture approach to working with aging adults. While I never entertained switching from school psychology to gerontology, it was helpful to know how agencies developed policy and what services were available. Several guest speakers came to the class, and one in particular hit a chord with me. He was the director of an assisted living facility in the area. He said the eldest daughter is most commonly the driver of caregiving for aging parents. That sunk in deeply, and I fully resonated with what he was saying. While I am the middle child, I also am the oldest daughter.

My father died at the end of July while I was still on summer break. My mother died seven weeks later in September. I took a leave of absence when my mother was put on hospice just after Labor Day, but she passed away rather quickly after my father died. It was the morning of her 83rd birthday. I learned it's not unusual for a spouse to pass away a short time after the other spouse dies. It took about three weeks after that to handle a lot of their business and to give myself some time to process my grief before I went back to work.

Three weeks wasn't enough time. I'm not sure there really is enough time to ever work through grief, and I'm not sure it ever goes away. I'll discuss more about the grieving process in another chapter; however, one important distinction to note when you are caring for a loved one is that grief begins long before the parent or loved one dies. In fact, once you start to take notice—or rather, become cognizant of—changes, differences, and deficits that point to diminished health or significant advances in aging, grief creeps in and takes up residence. It can show up as fear, anxiety, and often irritability and anger.

In the Sandwich Generation, someone always needs you, and they can easily become the recipient of your grief state. If you find yourself feeling extra grumpy, check in with yourself. Consider, "How do I feel about taking more and more care of my parents?" Ask yourself, "Is this grief disguised as something else?" Take time to talk with someone about your feelings. You can talk to a professional, your physician, a clergy member or faith leader, or seek out other caregivers. Most communities have caregiving support groups. While it's normal and natural to grieve when you become aware that the sun is closer to setting for your parents or loved one, walking through the world without support while grieving adds too much weight to your already laden shoulders.

I returned to my position as a school psychologist, and immediately people came out of the woodwork to tell me they were now in my shoes or to ask advice, because they saw their parents aging and they wanted to know what to do. I didn't have a lot of answers. I muddled through, doing what I thought had to be done, stumbling and guessing my way as best I could.

But people kept asking me about my experience, the process, how I managed things. Friends and co-workers who were now caring for parents sought me out. The day I returned to work, one person told me, "I'm in your shoes now." Another said, "We just put my dad on hospice." I became the person to tell about an ailing parent or new development in caregiving. Later, I decided to take a sabbatical from my school psych position and told people my intention to write this book. I heard, "I needed this book a year ago!" or "I'm going to need this very soon, and I know a lot of people who could use it right now." I started to do some serious research. I talked to people. I attended support groups. I found and joined online communities. I spoke to professionals in the field of gerontology.

I also began reflecting on what I did well and what I wished now that I had done differently. I explored the situation from a variety of vantage points (once a data geek, always a data geek). I zoomed in the lens to dig deeper and zoomed out to grasp the big picture. As time went on, I knew there were others with as much stress, confusion, compassion, resentment, and grief as I experienced. In several Facebook groups I offered thoughts. As I interacted with others and listened, I grew to appreciate how good I'd had it with my parents.

The thing is, I'd had it great. My parents and I got along. My siblings and I got along. My kids were doing great, and my husband was immeasurably helpful. My parents had saved well and had money to support themselves. They had done a lot to put things together so that the three of us kids, now adults, could be free to raise our own families. They were explicit that they never intended to live with any of us. They were set—they had money and long-term healthcare insurance.

This is most often *not* the case.

That doesn't mean it wasn't hard. It was. Even having money, there was a lot to manage. My dad had vascular dementia; my mother was diagnosed with Alzheimer's disease—not conditions they had planned for. My children kept growing up. Nothing was static. I was witness to the developmental processes of growing up *and* growing old.

As I looked closer and began to dissect and reflect, I began to realize I had skill to bring to the table. Initially, I thought I simply reacted and "felt" my way through, but as I started to look closer, I recognized that my years as a case manager with a variety of populations, as a school psychologist and as a disability advocate, had all come together to support me. I had internalized a lot of skills and knowledge that helped me anticipate needs and respond to crises both big and small. This was also true for many of my friends, colleagues, and connections in online communities. We all have talents and abilities that sometimes we aren't aware of until we need them. We often discount how strong we are, how much we know, how creative we are at solving problems, how good we are at networking to gather support, how much we can do.

What I also realized is there is no one right way to navigate the Sandwich Generation. Just as every sunset is different, everyone's story is unique. We each have our own private blend of chaos and calamity. And we each have our own superpowers.

## My Story

*The news of my mother's condition and my dilemma about going with my husband to take our son to college was not my first squeeze of the Sandwich, but it was a particularly painful one for me. One I'd feared would come.*

*In the end, after many tears, emotions ranging from frustration to sadness with side trips through anger and resentment, I finally quieted and listened to my heart. I conjured a conversation with my mother. What would she tell me if she were healthy, not grieving, and not fading with Alzheimer's?*

*I knew what she would say, because I knew that I was carrying forth her Legacy of Love for me. She would tell me to go with my son. For her, the choice would have been obvious.*

*I gathered as much information as I could from the physicians and nurses, and then I called everyone. My sister. My brother. I learned that my aunt and uncle would be in town during that time. My parents and my aunt and uncle were great friends for many years, so could they make time to come visit? Yes, of course, they could. My mother-in-law was already slated to stay with our daughter, a sophomore in high school. My sister could come for some of the time. People were willing to help, and I only needed to decide to go and then to ask.*

*It seems so simple. But in the throes of grief from my dad's passing, and now learning of my mother's grim return of cancer, nothing felt simple. Having your child move 2000 miles away for college is also not simple.*

*Every decision feels huge and overwhelming when you're in the Sandwich Generation.*

If you see yourself somewhere in my story, know that, while it's challenging, there are as many gifts as there are hurts, as much clarity as confusion, and more than enough moments of real joy and grace.

As I listened, learned, researched, and reflected, I felt a strong urge to share my stories, to share information, and to start a conversation. I now write the book I wished I'd been able to read when I went through the experience. I invite you to join me in the conversation, wherever you find yourself right now in this very complicated time inside the Sandwich Generation.

# "*We each have our own private blend of chaos and calamity.*"

# 2

# LIFE AND DEATH DISCUSSIONS

*How strange this fear of death is!*
*We are never frightened of a sunset.*

George MacDonald

Talking about death can be difficult. Suspicion and superstition surround the topic, and that makes it uncomfortable. "If I contemplate my parent's death, I may be willing it!" And if not willing it, it certainly feels morbid. But the truth is, we will all die one day. That is a certainty. Talking about it, considering what we want to do before our death, what we want to happen when we die, and making plans even though we can never know the exact day and time, can eliminate much of the fear often associated with death. It also helps those left behind, makes it easier to be fully present and helpful in those last days and moments.

When considering the end of our parents' lives, these conversations are critical. Primary care doctors attempt these discussions when a person is very ill or aging. Medical professionals often provide Advance Care Directives or other end-of-life questionnaires to determine what medical measures to take. For example, does the person wish to receive Cardiopulmonary Resuscitation (CPR) at any point? What about going on a respirator? What about a feeding tube?

What life-sustaining measures are acceptable? The law may require medical professionals to sustain life artificially if there is no Advance Directive. It can be painful for a spouse, sibling, child, or other friend or family member to make the decision to stop artificial life support. This dilemma can lead to painful family discord and possibly costly, extended legal battles.

Consider also what types of after-death procedures a parent might have wanted. If undecided, this becomes a potential source of family discord. Did your parent wish to be buried? If so, where? What type of service did they want, if any? Did your parent wish to be cremated? What if family members disagree about burial versus cremation? Again, a costly, extended battle can ensue.

Furthermore, what financial resources are available for end-of-life and after-death expenses? Who will bear the cost of those events?

Engaging in a discussion of these considerations and documenting the wishes and decisions creates space. It's a roadmap that provides peace and comfort. It can also bring families together rather than pulling them apart.

These discussions aren't easy, and there are people who don't want to talk about death. Maybe your parent isn't willing to discuss these matters with you. In that case, it might be helpful to converse with willing siblings as a way to head off discord. Getting ahead of conflict can ease difficulty later. I call this "front loading." When we talk about what might happen, what crazy curves might be ahead, we can reduce the stress when or if it appears. That sort of conversation looks at what might go right and what might go sideways, but imagining a possible contingency plan can bring focus to priorities. It's also an opportunity for family members to set intentions about what they want to happen.

Bottom line: Talking about something doesn't make it happen. Talking about pregnancy won't make you pregnant and talking about death won't kill you or anyone else.

But what if you don't have siblings, or the relationship with siblings is so impaired you can't imagine having the discussion? Then I highly recommend having the discussion as a clarity exercise with yourself.

Yes—talk to yourself! Get clear on what you envision for this time. How do you see yourself feeling, behaving, managing, and coping through the caregiving years? What are your priorities? What will you accept in terms of your time? What duties are you willing to take on? What areas or tasks do you already know you don't want to handle? Simply put, what are your boundaries around all of this?

In the next chapter is a self-assessment to clarify what YOU feel and think and are willing to do.

Think of it this way: Talking about death is an extension of talking about our life. Stories told through movies or books have a beginning, a middle, and an end, and all parts are essential. Without an ending, a movie or a book is incomplete. Sometimes we might not watch the end of a movie or read the end of a book, but it's still there. Not seeing it or reading it doesn't mean isn't there.

Just like sunsets (and sunrises, for that matter), even if we didn't see it, we know it happened.

Every life has an ending, and unlike with a book or movie, we can't skip it.

I thought a long time about how to craft conversation tips for death discussions. I needn't have pondered so long. I did what many folks these days do—I searched the web. There I found Death Café.

The Death Café movement was founded by Jon Underwood, who envisioned a place where people could meet to talk through their fear, curiosity, and any other feelings about death, to consider how to live in the present, and to share tea and cake.

Underwood had simple guidelines for Death Café. It must be a safe place with confidentiality; it must be free of charge; no one should be there to sell a service or materials; and there should be tea and cake.

:e—or other refreshments—are a means to nourish
ìharing food with each other, he believed, is an act of
ɔre, while talking about death, we can be more fully
_. ᵼᴜ ᵼne gift of life in the moment.

I attended a Death Café in my area, and the experience was enlightening. The facilitator was kind and gentle. People were allowed to share anything on their mind about death. Everyone was there for different reasons: Some were curious or fearful of death, several had experienced loss recently, one person had a terminal illness, and another lived with a life-threatening condition. Several others worked with people who were dying. There was no preaching or agendas. It was respectful and peaceful.

Overall in our society, we don't talk much about death. We focus a lot on being present, on being mindful, and that's good. What I found at Death Café was the coexistence of both. In fact, I found that being present to life made talking about death simple, elegant even. To talk about death is to talk about life.

Death Cafés are held in over 56 countries. Google Death Café to find one near you, or find a way to start your own. This is one way to get more comfortable with broaching the subject.

## Starting the Conversation—Your Own Death Café!

Ideally, as I've suggested, conversations with family, trusted friends, and possibly legal counsel are most helpful earlier rather than later. Long before anyone needs to know the specifics, there are several important things to consider when starting this conversation about death. It's also helpful to know that there will likely be more than one conversation about the topic. Be willing to circle back to it.

Who should be present in this conversation? Certainly, those who will be giving direct care, whether it is financial, legal, or physical, and of course, your parent or parents. Include a parent's partner if they're remarried or in another relationship. The first conversation may not delve into specifics; rather, it might simply open the door so that future conversations can happen. It's not a time for a lot of "shoulding"—"You should do this. You shouldn't do that." It's a time for exploration, since there are multiple right answers. Some people find this excruciating, and if you know this, or soon discover this, plan to circle back to it to get to specifics. The following outline is not intended for one long conversation, but may occur over time. The key is to manage your own mindset first.

- Prepare for the conversation—take as much time as you need here!

  o Take time to meditate, pray, ponder, or journal about your feelings FIRST. Acknowledging your feelings is essential.

    - What are your hopes for your parents?

    - What are your fears for your parents?

    - What feelings are you holding onto from childhood that could impact the conversation?

    - How might you let go of resentments right now?

  o Eliminate the word "should" from your questions or statements. The awful "should" can stop a conversation in its tracks. Don't "should" on yourself or others!

  o Replace "should" with "I'd like to understand how you feel about…"

  o What are the facts, the current status quo?

    - Health conditions?

    - Financial position?

    - Attitudes toward death?

  o Write out potential questions and think through how YOU would answer the questions for yourself. This puts you in a mindset of compassion and empathy.

- Consider whose presence is imperative to the conversation. Who needs to be there?

    - Sometimes less is more with respect to how many people participate. You can always invite others later.

    - Who is likely to be the day-to-day caregiver?

    - Who is likely to take on legal issues?

    - Who will take on healthcare advocacy?

    - Keep in mind, one person may serve in all roles.

- If possible, rehearse with someone first—a partner, spouse, friend, or even a geriatric social worker.

- The Initial Conversation

Enter the conversation consciously. Set an intention of compassion and inquiry. Ask what your parent wants, rather than what **should** they do.

- Schedule the conversation for an open time without competition for attention—not holidays, not before another event, not right after a doctor visit, not on Super Bowl Sunday.

- Listen and give time for answers.

- End the conversation with:

    - Gratitude

    - A plan to continue if needed

    - A plan to document at a future date

- Future Conversations

- Revisit areas of ambiguity. What wasn't clear or still seems fuzzy?

- Seek clarity and commitment.

- Envision the best possible future together.

- How can we partner with our parents to have the best image or version of their sunset?

- What feelings do we generate by our current behaviors with one another now, between siblings or between you and your parent.

- What behavior do we need to change in ourselves in order to generate positive feelings?

- Documentation

  o Most healthcare plans offer Advance Directives to document end-of-life wishes.

  o The Medicare.gov website offers guidance on Advance Directives.

  o Many states and many nursing homes, care homes, or assisted living facilities use the POLST form (Physician's Orders for Life Sustaining Treatment).

  o An organization called Five Wishes also has a good form available online for $5.00 (as of this writing) that is legally recognized in most states.

Bottom line—it is never too early to consider what a person wants for the end of life. Once we truly started caring for my parents, my husband and I discovered the truth of the old adage, "no time like the present." Since then, we've discussed it with our children. We formed a family trust and put our desires in writing. We both have Advance Health Care Directives (Living Wills). The webpage for National Institute on Aging, a department within U.S. Health and Human Services, provides a lot of information about the need for advance healthcare planning, as well as how to get started putting those wishes in writing. We felt strongly that we don't want our children to have to slog through all of that at the end of our lives. The lesson we learned is that we can take that burden from them now.

When is a good time to begin? My husband and I decided there is no time like the present to pass along this end-of-life strategy to our kids. They're now adults. We found a useful tool to help them each think about what they might want if they were to be seriously injured. We asked them to complete the Five Wishes form. They agreed, and each completed one. My daughter cried while writing hers, and I cried when I read them. I worried that I was asking too much, but she stopped me and said that even though it was hard to consider, she knew it was important. As always, my children are my teachers. She told me that I had to let her have her feelings, even if they were teary ones.

What we're talking about is end-of-life care, and what is striking is that the medical profession is not particularly adept or even well informed about end-of-life issues. Physicians focus on sustaining life for as long as possible and often by extreme measures. Talking about the end of life is outside of their purview.

In general, that's what we want from our physicians, isn't it? We see a doctor to cure illness, end pain, lead and coach us toward better health. Medical science has made enormous progress in treating illness and disease. But let's face it—they can prolong life, but they cannot "cure" aging or eliminate death. It's difficult for medical personnel to focus on the fact that we will all die, but is that a failure of medicine? Probably not.

It's also true that, in general, people live much longer now than ever before. This in and of itself creates a dilemma for society. People who live longer may not be able to continue working. We still think of retirement as sometime after age 65. As stated earlier, statistics for life expectancy as estimated in a 2018 Centers for Disease Control study suggest the average American will live to about age 78.7[7].

My own parents lived to be 83. My dad retired at 62 after a stroke. My Mom retired at 63 after nearly 20 years of teaching. Both lived an additional 20 years, and I am happy to say they lived with joy and in comfort after years of careful money management.

But in my own circle of family and friends, far more people are living to be 90 or older. Initially after my parents died, I admit I felt cheated when I heard of so many people living well into their 90s. But we hear about those folks because they are anomalies, not because they are the norm. Still, in my grief, it felt like a great loss that my folks only made it to 83, six years longer than the average and much longer than those on the other end of 78 who make up that average. It's all a matter of perspective.

Most enlightening for me as I researched material for this book is the focus on promoting an ethic of quality of life versus quantity of life.

What if, in discussing end of life with our parents and family, we focus primarily on the quality of life? How might that shift our discussions? How might that allow us to build a Legacy of Love for our parents, our children, and ourselves?

We need to discuss specifics about the degree of life-sustaining medical procedures we want, but we also need to talk about how we want to feel and what we want to do in our years. This is where emotional work to get clear on our own thoughts about death and about our relationships with our parents and siblings comes into play. This is where powerful healing can occur.

## My Story

*As I sit in the doctor's office with my dad, I am surprised to be so emotional. This is a routine visit to the nephrologist (kidney doctor), after all, simply checking in and reviewing labs. But the doctor surprises me. Everything looks like the prior visit, but the doctor wants to probe about what might be next.*

*I've gotten to know this doctor and his staff over the last year and really like them. They make me feel welcome and always thank me for coming with my dad, and they speak directly to him and not through* me to him, which I appreciate. Appointments have been on time and efficient.

My father's kidneys are not great, and he is edging that line where dialysis might be considered. I don't fully grasped that fact until the doctor brings it up at this appointment. For some reason—denial?—I thought that was a long time away. But the option looms on the horizon. I watch a video with my dad about the different options for dialysis. None look good. I don't think home dialysis will work unless my parents have an overnight nurse, since my mother with her Alzheimer's cannot be depended upon to help him. Coming for dialysis three days per week for three hours or more at a time also seems daunting.

I am taken aback when the doctor asks my dad if he wants to do dialysis at all.

"But won't he have to do something if his kidneys fail?" I ask.

"Dialysis is an option, but even the surgery to place the port for your father could be risky, considering his history of stroke. And while dialysis is not particularly painful, it isn't particularly pleasant either," he says.

He then looks directly at my dad and says, "I think we might want to consider the quality of your life at this point onward. How do you feel about that?"

"Yeah," says my dad. "I don't think I want to spend a lot of time with this kind of rigmarole."

I don't know what to say. I have just started taking a more active role in my parents' care, going to doctor visits and checking in on them at home, looking over bills and financial statements. I've only recently signed the papers to be appointed as their healthcare advocate. This is the first time it hits me that we are talking about the end of my dad's life.

The doctor takes time to talk more with my dad. He indicates that his numbers still look good and nothing is imminent, but he wants to know more clearly my dad's wishes, so that he can adjust meds accordingly.

*We end the meeting, and I load my dad into his transport wheelchair. I wheel him out to the waiting room and go back in to schedule the next appointment. As I look at possible dates with the doctor's assistant, I can't see my phone—it is a blur through my tears. I can't talk for fear I'll start sobbing. The assistant notices and hustles me into the exam room. The doctor comes in and asks what he can do.*

*"I didn't know we were so close. I didn't know we were talking about how he was going to die," I manage to say through tears.*

*"We don't know. But it's best we know what he wants. He's not a young man. Does he want to do this? Doesn't sound like it. We keep trying to extend life, and that's good; but at some point, we need to know what the person wants, especially at his age," he says quietly.*

*We exchange a few more thoughts. He is kind but clinical. I pull myself together, dry my eyes, blow my nose, and walk out to meet my dad and take him home.*

I shared this with my husband at the end of the day, and I was so grateful that this doctor had taken time to ask my dad a tough question. He'd given us a lot of information over the last few months, but now was the time to be specific and make decisions for ongoing care. It shifted my thinking about what was necessary for both my parents. We had discussed generalities about what was on the horizon, but now we needed to revisit the discussion and talk about their limits, what kind of life they wanted to live, and what would a "good day" feel like?

The experience underscored the necessity of circling back to the conversation.

It's not really talking about death and grief, I realized. These conversations are explicitly about LIFE and how each of us wants to live it.

**"These conversations are explicitly about LIFE and how each of us wants to live it."**

# 3

# MINDSET FOR THE SANDWICH GENERATION

*The strange thing about the sunset is that we actually don't want the sun to set, we want it to stay right on the horizon, not below it, not above it, just right on it!*

**Mehmet Murat Ildan**

What is your mindset as you find yourself in the Sandwich Generation or see it on the horizon, as you face the looming sunset?

Mindset is a set of beliefs and attitudes that inform how we react and respond to situations. In her groundbreaking book, *Mindset: The New Psychology of Success*, Carol Dweck, Ph.D. details how some people have a growth mindset, which is a belief that we can learn new things and overcome challenge, while others have a fixed mindset, which suggests this is just how we are and we cannot change a skillset. It's our belief about ourselves and our potential, so to speak. When we consider the daunting prospect of caring for aging parents while raising our own children, our mindset plays a huge role in how we move forward. What are the thoughts that dominate our attitude when we approach this often difficult task? Is there ambivalence?

Resentment? Fear? Grief? Sadness? Overwhelm? Worried we just aren't skilled in this area and never can be?

Beyond growth or fixed mindset, how we envision this journey—because it will be a journey of indefinite length, but ultimate resolution—can make a stunning difference in not only our well-being, but also the well-being of our children, family, and parents. Our mindset will govern how we approach the tasks ahead and what our children ultimately learn about challenge, support, compassion, and resilience.

Think about the added task of taking care of your parents while continuing to raise your children. Take a moment to breathe deeply, and then complete the following self-assessment. Consider each statement and rate yourself on a scale of 1 to 5, with 1 being "Strongly Disagree" and 5 being "Strongly Agree."

| | | 1. Strongly Disagree | 2. Disagree | 3. Neither Agree nor Disagree | 4. Agree | 5. Strongly Agree |
|---|---|---|---|---|---|---|
| 1. | I am emotionally ready and willing to take on this challenge. | | | | | |
| 2. | I understand my parents' current physical health needs. | | | | | |
| 3. | I understand my parents' current emotional needs. | | | | | |
| 4. | I am aware of my parents' current financial needs and am equipped to manage them. | | | | | |
| 5. | I am ready and able to balance raising my children while caring for my parents. | | | | | |
| 6. | I recognize that I am the one person who can do most of this work. | | | | | |
| 7. | I feel calm, loving acceptance of the tasks ahead. | | | | | |
| 8. | I have strong habits in place to take care of my emotional and physical needs. | | | | | |
| 9. | Right now in my life, I have the support I need to take on this challenge. | | | | | |
| 10. | Other family members are ready and willing to help me in this challenge. | | | | | |

Review your ratings and revisit these questions often. Your answers will change. Do common themes arise? Do you have more questions about WHAT to do than about your WILLINGNESS to take on the challenge? Do you have the support you need? Are other family members supportive of your efforts?

There are no right or wrong answers. These are measurement questions. I call them "yardstick questions." Where are you on the yardstick? You're not a bad person if each one made you tremble with doubt or fear or anger. You can't fail a self-assessment. Most of these items still give me pause.

In approaching the Sandwich Generation journey, it's important to take stock of your needs, both emotionally and practically. It's also essential to consider where on the yardstick you find yourself right now in terms of willingness and knowledge. Far too often, this life-changing situation simply falls into the lap of one person. There isn't an election. We don't get the chance to jump up and volunteer. We don't go through training and earn a certificate. We often get this task by default, because we live closest; we are the oldest or youngest; we are the only one; we are the "good" one who still talks to our parents. And frankly, in the United States, there are no laws stipulating that a child must care for an aging parent, although most do.

## So, however it falls to us, we do have a choice.

It's crucial to recognize that we have a choice, because when we understand that it *absolutely* is a choice and that we are free to make it, we can move on to own it, define it, set boundaries around it, and embrace it.

Acknowledgment that we are free to choose, and we actively do so, engages our personal power. This leads us to a growth mindset; we can learn what we do not yet know. To remain stuck thinking that we don't have a choice keeps us mired in a fixed mindset and victimhood. It renders us powerless.

Even when we accept the choice, significant challenges can

be stressful and frustrating. It's important to consider our current situation. I experienced a great deal of stress going through this time period. I thought a lot about what had stressed me out the most. I wasn't sure I knew what to do, who or what agencies could help me, and I was a full-time working mom with two kids. I spoke with a number of others who had gone through it or were now in the midst of it. I analyzed the comments on Facebook Groups for people in the Sandwich Generation. I chewed on all of that information and found that distress often runs along two paths: *Knowing* what to do (Knowledge Base) and *emotional strength* to do it (Stress Status).

## Knowledge-Stress Matrix

I am a visual processor. I want a graph or a picture, so I put together what I call the **Knowledge-Stress Matrix**. I conceptualized a grid much like a game board that identifies not just the two broad categories, Knowledge and Stress, but how my position—where I find myself—on each continuum impacts my parenting and family.

One continuum is **Knowledge Base**. How much knowledge do you have about caring for an elderly person? What skill set do you need? What resources are available? Do you know where to seek support and information? Talk about the need for a growth mindset—do we believe we can learn new skills and even overcome what we perceive to be our limitations?

The other continua are **Stress Status**. To some extent, everyone experiences stress. Some people have learned and adopted healthy ways to manage stress, or they have fostered relationships that provide emotional support. At a minimum, they have an idea of where to seek support for the emotional load that comes with caring for an aging parent. How about you?

Also consider the unique challenge in the Sandwich Generation. We are not simply caregivers to our parents; we are also in the midst of raising our children. Therefore, wherever we find ourselves within this matrix has a bearing on our children. We could say the challenge of parenthood runs along similar continua. We have to manage our knowledge base as well as our stress status. But as parents inside the Sandwich Generation, we are educating our children about how we view aging and caring for our elders. This is where we might ask, "What kind of legacy am I leaving for my children?" Legacy in this sense is more than money or property—it's the wisdom of how we approach life itself. What example are we setting?

Our children watch us and learn from us. What are we teaching them?

As humans we are always learning. Sometimes our learning is intentional, and sometimes it's unconscious or accidental. At times our children seem to be learning a lot more than we are! We think and hope that they learn from what we tell them, but often they learn by watching us and drawing meaning from that. Consider the child whose parents says not to lie, but then tells fibs and lies themselves within earshot of the child. Is it any surprise that a child learns that truth telling is situational or optional? Children learn from what we do more than from what we say.

## Systems

Beyond the two continua of knowledge base and stress status, we also need to consider what systems and routines we already have in place in our family, work, and social lives. In fact, are we aware of the systems or routines we're currently using? You might think you aren't using many systems, but in all likelihood, you have some things in place. How functional or effective those are might be another story.

Without getting too deep into systems theory, suffice it to say that humans are part of many systems. Systems theory suggests that every system is set up to produce the results it gets. But are we aware of what systems we are setting up? We might think we've set up healthy systems, but maybe not. For instance, if our intended goal is to lose weight and we buy packaged foods that proclaim to be "lo-cal" or "lite" and we buy cases of diet soda, and we don't lose a lot of weight, is it any wonder? A deep dive of self-reflection is important. We need to look at what works and what doesn't.

Examine your systems by looking closely at your routines and patterns. Humans tend to develop routines and patterns of behaviors to stay on track and to navigate through all the systems that surround communities of people. What ways have we found to maneuver through legal, medical, employment, and school procedures? We form carpools or time our commute so we can drop off the kids, get to work, pick up the groceries, get the kids to after-school activities, and so on and so on. We develop patterns to manage money or to stretch each paycheck beyond all limits. Some of these patterns or routines are helpful; some are not.

For many years my mindset was, "I can do it all myself." Even after getting married, I kept up my own pattern of doing it all: cleaning, cooking, walking my dog, planning social things. My husband was a lucky man, and he'd probably tell you that himself. With money management, though, I didn't have great systems. I'm not sure why I thought tossing bills to the side would ever be a great strategy—I didn't learn that from my folks—but I did it now and then. I'd pay the late fee, no problem, because the banks had good systems! I bought items on impulse rather than waiting for a sale or setting money aside, because the retailers and marketers had expert systems. The funny thing is, I married a starving actor in Los Angeles, and I'd had steady jobs for most of my life. While he figured out how to pay his bills on time from his patchwork of part-time jobs and had a pristine credit rating, I needed to repair my credit if we were ever going to have a family and buy a home. I needed to change my money habits. I had to look at my systems and the systems with which I interacted—banking and retailers—and be more aware.

Look at this framework and consider where you are in terms of **Knowledge Base** between Uninformed (I don't know what to do) and Informed (I have an understanding of what is needed) and **Stress Status** between High Stress (unmanaged stress) and Low Stress (strategies in place to manage stress.) Consider, too, that it's possible to move from one quadrant to the other if you stop to consider where you are. This is about mindset, and you can change your mindset, but only if you take time to examine it first and then set intentions for where you want to go and what kind of legacy you want to build for your children.

**Legacy of Chaos:** Uninformed and High Stress. We lack emotional stability, are frazzled by high stress, and we have no idea of what to do. Some stress may be related to caring for elders and some may be from other areas of life: work, marriage, children, health, or any number of other aspects of life. It's likely that we don't have a lot of strong systems in place. We might not have developed routines that work, are resistant to routines, or simply are not aware that we lack systems. This is a tough place. Stress is contagious, and we may be unintentionally passing stress along to our partners and children. I found myself here a lot in the beginning, and it crept up at other times, as well.

In the Legacy of Chaos, we are often in a state of "overwhelm." We struggle with even simple decisions. We rarely have time for ourselves in this space. There is so much to learn, and our ambivalence about being in this situation is palpable. We may be teaching our children that aging is overwhelming and unpleasant. We may not have the capacity to give them all that they need during this time.

Legacy of Resentment: Informed and High Stress. We have an idea of what to do, but we're frazzled and lack emotional support. Again, stress is contagious. It can infect our whole household and family. Not only can it inflict its own wounds, but the added toxin of resentment can fester quickly and impact relationships in the long term. Resentment often creeps in when our systems become inconsistent. Perhaps we're trying to pull it all together, but what used to work doesn't work now. Maybe we're trying to rely on others or feel others are laying all the responsibility at our feet, so we become inconsistent with our routines and systems trying to encourage others or fit others in.

Legacy of Resentment forms when we take on every task that comes our way, or we get frustrated that someone else doesn't know what needs to be done or how to do it, or even when they don't do it our way. We might ask ourselves, "Why me?" or "How come they don't know what needs to be done?" Our children are likely to learn that aging is unpleasant and older people are a burden. Sibling relationships may deteriorate. I found myself in the "Why me?" camp more than once because I didn't ask for help well or wasn't specific about what needed to be done. If someone jumped in to help but did it differently than I would have, I was irritated. My siblings lived far away, so daily help from them wasn't an option. I had to find other ways to leverage their willingness to help. I had to find ways to let go of the expectation that everyone knew what had to happen, could read my mind, and that my way of doing it was the right way.

Legacy of Obligation: Uninformed and Managed Stress. We don't know what to do, but we do have emotional supports in place. Obligation is not a poor place to be, but it lacks the added elements of joy and whole-heartedness. It may keep us from seeing all the gifts of compassion that come from caregiving of any kind. It just feels heavy. Another weight on our shoulders. Our systems often appear incongruent here. We have them—we've developed some good routines—but they don't match the new needs in our lives. They're incongruent and fail to take the load off, which is what they're meant to do.

A Legacy of Obligation emerges when we have no idea what to do but we are willing to do it anyway—we at least accept our "fate." We muddle through somehow but are fearful of what we're facing due to lack of knowledge. It's a scattered feeling or a heavy feeling because we are slogging through. Our uncertainty frightens us and our children. Our children might learn that aging is scary and something to avoid. They might feel scared around older people. I felt this way many times because, just like children grow and change, aging parents change. Nothing is static.

Legacy of Love: Informed and Managed Stress. We know what to do and we have the emotional bandwidth to do it. Look, it's never easy, but getting to a place where we can manage our stress levels with support from others and a commitment to caring for ourselves, as well as leveraging the knowledge and expertise of others, can be a priceless gift to a family. As we adjust, our routines and systems evolve. We actively try new routines after taking time to consider our family's needs.

Love has a place in all areas of the framework, but what's most visible to others? A Legacy of Love develops when we've figured out a healthy means to manage stress and feel somewhat competent in what we are doing, or at least know how to marshal resources and support to help us. Our love for both our parents and children shines through. Here our children are likely to learn that aging is natural, even if it's hard, and we demonstrate how to care for others in concrete ways. In fact, our behavior trains our children how to care for us someday. They learn how to accept a challenge and grow from it. They see us caring for our own well-being in active and healthy ways. We will have down days, but we demonstrate resilience.

Is it possible to move from one quadrant to the Legacy of Love space?

Yes! We can work on our mindset and move towards a Legacy of Love at any time. In fact, I have floated around from quadrant to quadrant. When I became aware that I needed to fortify support or learn something new, that prompted me to assess my mindset and make necessary changes. I didn't do this once. I did it over and over, and I use this matrix for other areas of my life even now. We can learn from others, seek resources, and develop strategies to face the challenges. Every situation is different. There is no one-size-fits-all, but there are ways to adapt solutions.

Information is attainable. Simply by picking up this book you are beginning to fill in the holes of information. Where can I find this? How might I handle that? See the Resource section in the back with information and contacts for many areas associated with caregiving, managing information, self-care, parenting, the grief process, and beyond. The challenge is to identify first what you know you don't know. Write down questions and put them into categories. Categories might be:

- Healthcare

- Legal

- Financial

- Residential/housing

- Self-care

- Parenting

- Hospice

- Funerals

- Grief

- Family relationships (siblings, marriage).

Once you have identified what you believe you need to know, you can check off a category at a time. This book is divided into sections that address many of those areas, and the Resources section has itemized referrals for each.

You can learn what you need to know, and you can find people to help you with what you can't do.

Bolstering emotional stability is a bit less concrete, but it's absolutely attainable. It may require letting go of some habits and developing new ones. The most important habit to develop, if you don't already have it, is to put yourself first. This book contains a chapter called "Ruthless Self-Care." Taking care of yourself is essential, not just for you, but for all those you care for.

It may also mean letting go of toxic people in your life. There are people who "need" you: your children, your partner, your parents. There are people who are not equipped to help you to the extent you think they "should." There are people you tend to carry in your life—at work, in your neighborhood, in a friend group, in your family. You probably can't carry them now, and they might not understand that. They will hold on, and it can weigh you down.

So, what do you do?

## Detaching with Love

Prior to having children and working as a school psychologist, I worked in Los Angeles with at-risk populations. I developed and administered several programs that served people who moved from the street to housing. Many had alcohol or drug addiction or mental health disorders. I learned about the 12 Steps from Alcoholics Anonymous and about co-dependency. This is where I learned the concept of "loving detachment." Melody Beattie, one of the foremost co-dependency and recovery specialists in the country has written many books on the subject. She describes "loving detachment" as the ability to recognize our unhealthy patterns of trying to control another person with our reactions. We react with anger, shame, guilt, hurt as a way to convince someone we love not to do something we believe is harmful to them or to us. We try to manipulate them into doing what we think they "should" with our emotions or passive aggressive behaviors. But it doesn't work. It keeps unhealthy patterns going. Detaching with love means moving away from the episode. Take a walk. Don't engage in the argument. Don't reply to the text or call immediately. Be realistic in your expectations of others. Take care of your needs first.

It sometimes means letting people go.

It might feel brutal or insensitive, but taking care of your needs and not getting swallowed up by others' needs who are not on your priority list is the most loving thing you can do as a parent for your children and a caregiver for your parents.

Imagine someone is threatening or upsetting your child, or your child is sick. You will do almost anything to intervene or find help. You will nurse your child back to health no matter what, and you would do what it takes to make sure your child felt safe.

But do you do that for yourself? If you don't, who does? Who knows better than you what you need—even when you think you don't know what you need?

The point is, putting yourself first is essential. There are ways to reduce stress, keep healthy, and generate energy. Some people think self-care is, well, selfish. But self-care is the ultimate act of love for others, because if you fall apart, who else suffers? It's not only you. Taking care of yourself increases your ability to fully care for others in a healthy manner. In addition, your children learn by watching you. They learn that self-care is essential. It teaches resilience in a concrete way.

As I mentioned earlier, stress is toxic and is often associated with disease. I also mentioned the study that suggested caregivers often demonstrate increased longevity rates as compared to others not in a caregiving role. This was an interesting contradiction to other studies that demonstrated increased stress experienced by caregivers leads to increased health problems in the caregiver group. Stress often is an underlying cause of disease. However, this study and several similar studies demonstrate positive benefits of family caregiving that counteracts the stress! Caregiving leads to higher levels of psychological distress, *but* the act of caregiving also creates a buffer to the effects of distress through small but consistent acts of compassion. The act of caregiving can neutralize the detrimental effects of high stress and psychological distress.

Let's think about that. If caregiving can benefit health and longevity, it likely stems from voluntary and loving acts. Yes—it's more work, frustrating work; but work that is conducted willingly and with an open heart is more beneficial than acts taken out of resentment or chaos or duty.

Coping is important for well-being. Coping is essential if we are to move through difficult times. And science shines a light on the physical and emotional benefits of coping strategies such as meditation, exercise, gratitude, and even compassion.

Our bodies produce oxytocin, often called the "cuddle hormone," when we engage in pleasing social situations and acts of compassion.

Mothers produce oxytocin during labor and lactation. Men produce oxytocin also, and it's thought to promote social awareness in humans. Studies indicate that consistent, small acts of compassion are powerful producers of oxytocin. Our compassionate acts need not be grand gestures; the daily little things we do to care for others heals us.

Knowing that caregiving is beneficial for us as well as others suggests we will do well to care for ourselves in order to better care for those we love.

If you have any doubt about the importance of self-care, think again. Taking time for self-care has been practiced by some of the greatest caregivers the world has known. Mother Teresa, arguably one of recent history's most notable caregivers, insisted that her nuns and staff take off an entire year every four years. She knew that her caregivers needed to rejuvenate, replenish, and renew. Since caring for an aging parent can last many years, taking time off now and again and developing healthy strategies in everyday work is a no-brainer. We have to do it not only for our sake, but for the sake of everyone we love.

## My Story

*It is early April of 2015. The facility where my mom and dad live calls to say my father has fallen and broken his hip. I spend a day in the emergency room and later a hospital room getting all the necessary information and talking with doctors, all the while attempting to comfort my mother, who has a great deal of trouble fully understanding what has happened. Her long-term memory is fairly good, but Alzheimer's disease has greatly impacted her short-term memory. I feel distressed explaining my dad's condition over and over. All she wants to know is when he is coming home.*

*Coming home is not the first step. We have to consider his immediate needs. My dad will need surgery, but with his history of stroke, high blood pressure, and an assortment of other conditions including vascular* dementia, that is a huge risk for him. As his healthcare advocate, I have to give permission for surgery, because he cannot. He hates hospitals and only wants to go home.

After consulting with the anesthesiologist, my husband and I talk, pray, cry, and I may even scream and curse. Undergoing anesthesia is the biggest concern. He might not survive. But without the surgery, he will be in constant pain. On top of that, the surgeon is clear about the prognosis for a person in my dad's condition. He doesn't think my dad will live a year.

This is happening five weeks before my son will graduate high school.

My dad survives the surgery, but he cannot go back to the assisted living facility where he and my mom have lived for the last year and a half. They can't provide the care he needs. My mom can stay, but he will need a nursing-home level of care. But I have to have them together! My mom is disoriented in his absence, and he is disoriented without her. I could rent an apartment for them and hire 24-hour care. I could move my 15-year-old daughter into a room with my 18-year-old son to free up a room in our three-bedroom home, or I could put two hospital beds in the living room. Or I could find another place for them both.

My parents purchased a long-term healthcare plan nearly 20 years ago. It provides for assisted living, board and care, or nursing home care. It doesn't provide for in-home care. Consequently, this is one of the financial issues for me to manage as their financial power of attorney. Do I drain their savings or find a way to continue to use the long-term healthcare plan they purchased? Tough choices!

We decide to move them both and we find a more suitable place— one that provides excellent memory care and a much higher level of physical care. It comes with a higher price tag, but the insurance company approves the facility.

My dad has to spend two weeks in a nursing home, however, and graduation day approaches. I speak with the nursing home staff about *this. They say it is up to the insurance company as to when my dad will be released. My son will graduate on a Saturday, and I get a call the Friday morning before graduation that my dad will be released that afternoon. Family is coming in from everywhere, my son's Baccalaureate Mass is imminent, and graduation will be the next morning. I am so furious and frazzled I can hardly contain myself!*

*To add to this, it is the busiest time of year for me as a school psychologist. Since my dad's decline five months previously, I have carefully orchestrated the timing of meetings and reports to be sure I have room to breathe. And now I have to figure out how to move my mom and dad into a new facility and make sure he has the care he needs with a new staff. The timing couldn't be worse.*

*I drop back and punt. I arrange for my dad to privately pay for an additional four days at the nursing home. Once again, the balancing act between my own children's needs and my parents' needs confront me. I feel enormous stress at the end of May and early June. I honestly believe I will break.*

*My husband has a business trip planned for mid-June. We were going to join him and make it a family vacation. I consider cancelling so I can ensure a smooth transition for my parents and that they have all the services they need. Plus, I worry my dad might not make it. The surgeon's words ring in my ears. How much longer does he have? But my kids need me too, and our oldest child graduating high school deserves to be celebrated before he goes off to college. What should I do?*

In the end, we decided to take the trip. Both of my siblings had made plans to come in for a few days, stay at our house and take on visiting mom and dad. I needed the break before I broke. I needed to replenish for whatever the future held, not just for my dad but for my own family.

While I still sometimes feel a pang of guilt over going on vacation, I also remember that trip as one of our best vacations as a family. That time was great for all of us and we needed it.

Creative problem-solving. Leveraging resources, both money and people. Ruthless self-care. All of these came into play. Reflecting on all the discussions I'd had with my parents about their priorities and values ("We paid a lot for that insurance, Christy") helped me to do the best I could. It may not have been perfect, and I was often short-tempered and a bit crazed. But in hindsight, I think my children learned positive lessons and knew I gave my best. I was building a Legacy of Love.

# "I needed the break before I broke."

# 4

# PARENTING AS A CAREGIVER

*No matter who you are, what you've accomplished, what your financial situation is—when you're dealing with a parent with Alzheimer's, you yourself feel helpless. The parent can't work, can't live alone, and is totally dependent, like a toddler. As the disease unfolds, you don't know what to expect.*

**Maria Shriver**

## My Story

*"Christy, I think your mom is having memory problems. Have you noticed?" my Aunt asks me. Lately, a lot of people have been asking me this. No, I tell them. It's anxiety. She's just so worried about my dad. She worries all the time and is afraid to leave him for very long, so she cancels things she used to do. She has been cancelling book club, volunteering, and social engagements. But the question nags at me. Is it anxiety, or is something else going on?*

*My mom tells me, "I'm afraid I am more like my mother than my father!" She refers to her mother who died the day before her 80th* birthday, who probably had some form of dementia for years. She would walk around her home with a burning cigarette with a five-inch ash at the end, my grandfather following behind with an ashtray trying to keep the house from burning down. Her father lived nearly another 20 years and died at age 99. His memory was as clear as a bell, although he did tell me the decades seemed to blur together. My mom worries a lot about my dad, but she worries a lot about her memory, as well. Should I worry, too?

At this point I've been working as a school psychologist for ten years. Prior to that I developed and managed transitional housing programs for people and families who were homeless. I've worked with adults and children. I've worked with people with mental illness. I know anxiety when I see it, I tell myself. This is anxiety. But my conscience gnaws at me. Am I in denial? Sometimes we are most dangerous when we think we know things.

I visit my parents to touch base, and I check that my dad's pillbox is full for the week. I've been monitoring this recently, because Mom tells me Dad messes it up after she fills it. He's on a lot of medication. I look, and sure enough, pills have been moved and everything is a jumble.

"Who changed everything?" I ask them both. I sound like my mom did as a third-grade teacher for 25 years, interrogating the nine-year-old about the messy classroom or missing markers. The pillbox management bugs the crap out of my dad, who tattles. "She keeps messing with it." She is ratted out again and looks aghast and indignant. Seriously—is this what it has come to? I pull back from my frustration about having two more "children" to care for. Eventually, I fix the pills and tape a sticky note to the front: "Do not move, remove, or add any pills until you call Christy first." Yeah, that'll work, I tell myself.

Literally the next week I am in the same predicament. Exasperation sets in and I fix the pills again. This is crazy—do I need to come here three times a day to give my dad pills? Can I hire someone to come in to administer meds? Is that even a thing? I am certain it's a thing, but *what is the cost? I can see blowing through all their savings in a short amount of time hiring a bevy of caregivers to come in and out. Perhaps their insurance will cover this cost. I commit to investigating their policy. It's another to-do on my growing list of to-dos.*

One of the most difficult issues I faced while caring for my parents was becoming aware of how much I didn't know about how to care for them and how much my relationship with them changed. It's disorienting to realize you have become the parent to YOUR parent.

I think I had an idea that my parents would never really change and that they would always be the lively, fun, witty parents from my childhood. My father had a stroke around age 60, before I was married and had children. He lost his sharp wit and some of his confidence after that. He also lost his job earlier than expected. This diminished him in ways many older people face, typically men from this "Silent Generation." But he persevered and moved with my mom from Ohio to California to live in an active senior area to golf and travel and have fun. They did have fun, too. My dad had always been an avid golfer, and after her retirement from teaching for 20 plus years, my mom became an avid golfer as well. Always a popular and energetic woman, my mom was a member of several community groups. They were active in their church. She volunteered for community organizations. And they both doted on their grandchildren. My brother's two sons were grown and living in Michigan, but I had one young child, my son, and my daughter was born shortly after they relocated. Also, my husband and I relocated from Southern California to Northern California to be closer to them. Not long after I had my children, my sister had two girls, and they lived about two hours away—which is nothing in California commute time. My parents were highly involved. Very active. Very happy. And then they aged, slowly at first and then quickly at the end. To see them deteriorate and then degenerate as described in my story above was painful for me. And recognizing changes in our relationship was difficult. I didn't want to "parent" my own parents.

My challenge became taking on the role of helping them, maintaining healthy boundaries, and finding a way to treat them with the regard and respect they deserved from me. In other words, I had to learn how to care for them without treating them like toddlers.

## Parenting Children vs. Supporting Parents

Are we "parenting" our parents, or is it another dimension in the relationship? There isn't a great deal of literature along this line. Most articles identify this conundrum as particularly difficult, but the dynamic of the relationship hasn't been identified as a stretch on the continuum of human development.

A family friend whose father was in late stages of Alzheimer's disease told me she was frustrated when people tried to console her by suggesting, "He's not your father anymore." While the comment was likely offered with best intentions, she bristled. "He is still my father!"

While we hear about that spry 95-year-old who is as alert now as when he or she was at 30, most humans will experience some level of diminished capacity in terms of mobility, control of bodily functions, mental alertness, and judgment. It really does appear that as we age we go from dependent to independent to dependent again. We start life wearing diapers and we seem to end life wearing them too. For those of us caring for aging parents, from an emotional standpoint, it's damn difficult to buy adult diapers alongside your toddler's pull-ups.

Feelings of anger, disgust, sadness, despair, confusion, and even humor can enter the picture for the caregiver. This is normal. We are human, and our reactions, whatever they may be, are normal. It's irrational to expect to witness this tremendous shift in our parents' abilities and **not** experience strong emotions. We need to be gentle with ourselves, because this is hard. We are socially conditioned to recognize the changes in our children. There are countless parenting books, endless tomes on child development to alert us to our children's changing needs in body, mind, and spirit. There are books on the aging process, but we don't tend to devour those with quite the same speed. Perhaps it's too hard emotionally to explore. So, we must be gentle with ourselves.

We need to check our mindset. When we can rationally acknowledge that this is in fact normal and expected and something we, too, will likely experience, we can start to shift from feeling overwhelmed, sad, disgusted, or angry to acceptance.

I recall the first time I had to buy diapers for my dad. Such mixed feelings! I experienced shame at the register, hoping the checker didn't think they were for me. I think I made a comment about getting them for my dad, but likely the checker at Costco didn't particularly notice any item in my stash. But I felt so strange buying them. Then I thought about my dad. How hard must it have been for him to ask me to pick them up? I recall a time my mother had me pick up some Poise panty protectors for her. She was so sheepish in asking for them. She made a pretty big deal about indicating they were *"not diapers, but panty protectors."*

I also had to contend with their diminished judgment or social skills. My father seemed to lose his filter as he aged. He didn't seem to monitor his thoughts and consider what he should or should not say out loud, much like a young child. One night, my family took our parents out to dinner, and my dad used a derogatory term. I hissed to him across the table, "Dad! That's inappropriate. People don't talk like that anymore. Please don't use that language in front of the kids." And then he wore a shameless grin! On another occasion, again at a restaurant, when the server placed his meal in front of him, he complained loudly about how no one made grilled cheese sandwiches the right way anymore. Where did white bread go? Why did it have to be a sandwich? I started to be concerned about taking him out in public. It reminded me of when my son was two and became agitated and over-stimulated at a restaurant and needed time away after hurling the salt and pepper shakers across the table. Was I going to put my dad in time out?

Eventually I came to accept this as part of the process. It was a new normal for my parents. I had to change my relationship with them to meet their needs. While their behavior frustrated me, I didn't need to speak to them in a childish manner. I could speak to them in respectful tones. And I needed to put some of my school psych know-how to use.

## The Function of Behavior

One of the concepts from school psychology that helped me the most with this changing relationship was determining the function of behavior.

When a student was having difficulty in class or at school (playground, lunchroom, P.E.), teachers and administrators often asked me to observe and make recommendations. If the case was particularly challenging or ongoing, I might conduct a full functional behavior assessment (FBA) in order to develop a plan to support the student. While I didn't conduct an FBA on my parents, I did consider some of the factors I might use in an assessment with students.

In fact, applied behavior analysis, the theoretical foundation for functional behavior assessment and behavior therapy, is a growing field in gerontology.

Simplified, it goes something like this:

- **Setting Events.** What conditions might explain the behavior or set him up for an outburst or change in behavior? Was dad ill? Had he had a poor night's sleep? Was he taking or not taking prescribed medications? Was there recent trauma or changes to his routine? Did he have a urinary tract infection (a common precursor to changes in behavior)?

- **Consider the A B C's:** Antecedents, Behavior, and Consequences.

o   *Antecedents.* What happened just prior to the behavior? We could also call these "cues" or "triggers" to behavior. For instance, was it the time of day, place, people around him, something someone said or did?

o   *Behavior.* The challenging or "problem" behavior. What actually happened that was problematic? Not what you think was going on in the person's head, but actually what behavior occurred.

o   *Consequences.* We could also call these the rewards. What did my parent get following the behavior? Attention? A tangible object? Punishment? Something else?

In general, humans do what works. Because they don't have words or other means, infants and young children cry and have tantrums to get wants or needs met. They point and sometimes take our hand to lead us to what they want. They do what works and that trains us, which is not bad or wrong. But as they grow, we help them learn words and other behaviors that are more effective. As I watched my parents grow older, I found they lost some of their words and sophistication, as well. It seemed being socially appropriate was simply too much work.

Recognizing this concept gave me perspective. It helped me to find compassion for the challenges. And it gave me some distance. I felt less shame and frustration. I also felt less sadness. I realized that this is part of human nature and an aspect of the type of dementia my father had, which manifested as diminished social skills. That may sound too clinical for some people, but for me it was comforting. Holding that perspective, much like I did with my kids throughout their developmental stages, I found it easier to respond from a place of love and acceptance.

I also became acutely aware of how my way of talking with my parents changed over time. Just as I changed the way I spoke to my children over the years—cooing to them when they were infants, using a sing-song voice, engaging them as toddlers with rhymes and songs, becoming more concrete yet more complex as they grew from school-aged to teens and then to young adults—my language and communication changed with my parents. In some ways I reverted to that concrete language I used with younger kids. Being subtle didn't seem to work. The cognitive deficits were apparent with my parents, who both had some level of dementia in their last years. With my dad's vascular dementia and my mom's Alzheimer's, I felt the need to use the teacher voice I used with younger children, or children with impaired memories or cognitive functioning. Direct, specific, and short sentences. This is different than "talking down" to someone. It's about being concrete and non-judgmental. Say it simply. Use a neutral voice. Be respectful of time and place. If I had to address something of a delicate nature, like hygiene or medical issues, I did it privately, but I still did it. I found that if I didn't do this, then sometimes their needs might not be fully met by the staff of the assisted living facility or even by their doctor. I had to build a relationship with the professionals who cared for them, so that I could fill in information I knew my parents couldn't recall or that they didn't think was relevant. I had to do that as a parent when my kids were little—and I had to do it for my parents now.

## Communication

One of the major dilemmas in the Sandwich Generation is how we communicate with our families—our siblings, children, and parents. Communication is fundamental to keeping all the moving parts working together. But how do we move from the space of being our parents' child to exerting authority or influence over them? If we fear being disrespectful, are we in danger of not having essential conversations?

Here's what I've heard from a number of people:

- That's my parent. I can't tell them that.

- I'm still their child.

- I don't have the right.

- I am not comfortable.

- They won't listen to me.

- That would make them angry.

- That would hurt their feelings.

Somehow, we are thrust into a position where we have to adjust our tone, our willingness to talk about delicate issues, or our willingness to be more assertive or give direction. It's disorienting. Yet, we might be the best people to engage in these conversations. We see more and we know more. But it's important to consider *how* we engage in these conversations.

## My Story

*From talks with others on this journey, it appears that one of the most difficult and early conversations is about the car keys.*

*I feel in a strange sort of Twilight Zone while simultaneously discussing driving with my teenage son and his grandparents. It is mind boggling and painful. Copious tears are shed. I specifically talk with my dad about his driving. He has difficulty walking due to severe plantar fasciitis and diminished motor skills overall. He's had cataract surgery but still has vision problems. Yet he continues to drive from his home in a retirement community up to a local Starbucks. "I'm just going a few blocks!" he insists. But I fear he might take out a few golf carts along the way. I am also concerned that other drivers have become distracted over the years. My dad, unaware of new technology, doesn't share my concerns. He is certain he is fine. And besides, he says, my mother does all the long-distance driving.*

*I ask myself, "Who am I to tell my father he can't drive?" I write to his doctor to ask that he advise my dad to take a driver's test, and he does. Of course, my dad passes. Many senior drivers do pass the short, neighborhood drive with a DMV evaluator, if they are even asked to take a road test. (Some DMVs only require a written exam, as would happen later for my mother, who would fail it twice. Finally, they let her take the test verbally, and she passed. She'd complained that the wording was too difficult, and that sort of blew my mind. If she couldn't make sense of the written words, then how could she be deemed fit to drive? She is a native English speaker, so we're not talking about translation issues.)*

*I sit my dad down and share with him how grateful I am for his patience in teaching me to drive so many years ago. I remind him how he helped all three of us kids learn to drive and how he always emphasized being a defensive driver, because we could not anticipate what another driver might do. We had to be alert and prepared. I try to laugh with him about how he complained about older drivers back then, as I ease into the final point—he is likely that older and dangerous driver himself.*

*I haven't come to that awareness overnight. I've driven with him. I've paid attention to his reaction times. I know he has great instincts as a driver, but slower reaction times due to age and mobility. I also am aware of how much not driving will impact his life—he will lose his independence. No more private time away from home on his own to shop or discover something of interest. This is happening long before Uber or Lyft become common, and neither parent is particularly savvy with cell phones, let alone apps. Taxis are available, but quite expensive. There is public transportation, but not easily accessible. There are some senior transportation services, but not frequent, and the planning time alone would impact his feeling of independence. So, I know this is a major milestone and a painful one. I gather schedules and phone numbers of services, and I am willing to offer my availability to sweeten the pot.*

*As the conversation moves along, I start to cry. I tell him I know I cannot prevent him from driving. I don't have the right to take away his keys. But I implore him to consider not that he might hurt himself, but* *that he would be devastated to hurt another person. **Then, I set a firm boundary that he cannot drive my children.** If he continues to drive, then, so be it. But I don't feel safe with him driving my children. I know that hurts his feelings, but I have to set that boundary as much for him as for them. He thanks me for being honest. He doesn't commit one way or another, but about a month later he finally gives it up.*

*I don't know for sure if this conversation was the turning point, but I suspect it was a strong catalyst.*

That was one of the hardest conversations I had with my father. I tried to approach it by being straightforward, speaking to him with respect, acknowledging I knew it was hard for him as well as me, and then leaving him with the choice. No threats. It wasn't really a threat to tell him he couldn't drive my children, because he rarely did so, and this would impact me more than him. I didn't want to wait until something terrible happened to have the conversation. When it was clear to my husband and me that we were scared to be in the car when he was driving, we knew it was time. Waiting for a possible injury to himself or another person didn't seem like a responsible option. Before initiating the conversation, I discussed it with my brother and sister. Since both lived out of state and rarely had the opportunity to be in the car when he was driving, they graciously took my word for it. I felt empowered by their support.

Your conversation will probably be different. While the conversation is hard, it's easier than dealing with an accident that might have been prevented.

> **"***I had to learn how to care for them without treating them like toddlers.***"**

# 5

# THINK LIKE A
# CASE MANAGER

*Your eyes are blinded with your worries; you cannot see
the beauty of the sunset.*

### Jiddu Krishnamurti

During this Sandwich Generation journey, you will wear many hats: nurse, financial planner, legal aide, cook, therapist, you name it. In the sunset of your loved one's life, you also become the director as the stars move toward the horizon at the end of the film. You can take all of it on yourself or try to assemble a team using the resources at hand. And when you assemble a team, it's important to have a case manager—one person who manages the group.

As I've said, in my professional life, I've been a case manager or casework supervisor in a variety of communities. With my parents, using that framework helped me leverage resources for them more effectively. I didn't have to do it all, but I needed to know what was going on so that the different doctors and resource folks were not working at cross-purposes. I recall the moment I figured this out. I was at my wit's end with juggling different doctors, the assisted living facility, the skilled nursing facility, lawyers, and extra help I had hired to support my parents, who had a lot of needs. I plopped, with petulance, in the office of the director of the assisted living facility and declared, "I need an IEP for my parents!"

## Develop a Plan

For me, case management and specifically special education became a framework that helped me help my parents.

What's an IEP? Simply put, it is an Individual Education Program (or plan) designed specifically for students with special needs offered through the public-school system and mandated by the Federal Individuals with Disabilities Education Act or IDEA. Public school systems do their best to meet the needs of all students. For a student with special needs that impact learning, parents, teachers, and a specialist meet as a team to chart the best course forward. First, the team evaluates the supports that have been tried. If general education supports have not been successful, or if there are other factors (too numerous to mention here), the team may conduct an evaluation to determine eligibility and to explore what might be getting in the way of academic progress. Every member of the team gathers to discuss assessments, present levels of functioning, describe needs, and design goals to address those needs and methods for progress monitoring. It isn't perfect, but it's a good model for getting everyone who interacts with the student on the same page and working in concert toward agreed-upon goals.

Special Education is not perfect by any means. Other case management plans might not be perfect, either. But case management *does* promote a team approach to problem solving, and it calls for clear, unbiased evaluation to determine needs and to work toward agreed-upon goals. Case management plans are generally fluid and change as needed. A good plan provides a map for moving forward. For the plan to work, it's important to have current assessments from physicians and service providers in order to clearly identify needs. It's important to look at the big picture to identify specific needs that might be required. Parents or adult children caring for parents sometimes see only the struggle, or they make excuses for the struggle. I think of how I was in denial about my mother's memory. Assessments from unbiased professionals can help us better see the strengths and weaknesses of our loved one and learn what might be best going forward.

Keep in mind, though, many health or rehabilitation case managers are working to remediate deficits or concerns. If a person is injured and enters a rehabilitation center and receives physical therapy and occupational therapy, the goal is often to get the patient back to previous levels of functioning. A well-conditioned athlete who is injured is working to get back to competitive levels. In school settings, some students need accommodations, but don't need a fully modified curriculum in order to succeed.

## So, what we are working toward for our parents?

While it's important to have a plan, it's also important to know what all of us are working toward.

Quite frankly, there is no cure for aging.

For my parents, and for me, a safe and happy quality of life for them seemed to be the best goal.

There are conditions and illnesses that can't be reversed. Progressive illnesses like Alzheimer's may eventually be cured, and there are some medications currently on the market that can slow the disease's progression. But ultimately, as we care for our aging parent, spouse, friend, or other aging loved one, we have to grapple with end-of-life issues.

It's important to identify current levels of functioning and get a sense of how an aging parent is progressing toward the end of their life.

Remember those critical conversations? Those are part of this concept of case management. What can we glean from those talks that will help us case manage? This is where the fruits of those conversations can guide us. In what way can we support them?

I needed a cohesive plan for my parents. The director was great—she knew exactly what I was talking about, as she had an adult daughter with special needs and had spent many years in IEP meetings. We spoke the same language, and it made a huge difference.

My parents had done a great job of alerting my siblings and me regarding their desires about a lot of things such as assisted living versus in-home care. They had a trust and a will set up long before they were needed. They'd purchased a plan with the Nautilus Society that provided for cremation, a choice they made. They wanted to have their remains go to the nearest National Cemetery, since my dad had served during the Korean War. They were planners and savers, and that alone was a huge gift to me and my siblings.

I knew a lot about their desires and goals. But as I've said, my professional life has included some level of case management, so I naturally and organically pulled together a plan—not perfect, but a plan, nonetheless.

There is a growing field called Geriatric Care Management. I suspect this field will grow in number and availability considering the continued aging of the Baby Boomer generation. If you can find a case manager, and if your parents or family can afford those services through insurance or private pay, I highly encourage you to search them out. There are also national associations that can help you find providers in your area that deal with disease-specific resources and aging resources. See the Resources section at the back of the book for some options. You can also query your parent's doctor or medical provider to determine whether his or her health plan includes case management services or referrals.

Above all, advocacy is important. Knowing more about how case management works can help you find the right fit with an agency or help you take on some of the management if you cannot afford or find the right service.

What exactly is case management, and what does a case manager do?

On their website, the Commission for Case Manager Certification defines case management as "a collaborative process of assessment, planning, facilitation, care coordination, evaluation and advocacy for options and services to meet an individual's and family's comprehensive health needs through communication and available resources to promote patient safety, quality of care, and cost effective outcomes." Many hospitals have case managers on staff to assist patients and families with care. Many health insurance companies also provide case managers. If your parents' plan or medical group has case management services, I highly recommend contacting them to use their service.

Applying principles of case management takes a load off you. It's also better for your parent. Aligning all providers with your parents' needs and expressed wishes and goals can save time, money, and worry. If you're checking in with a team, you're not scrambling to do it all yourself. If you have a plan, if you have goals, then you have a clearer sense of what is working and what is not. It's easier to adjust your course. It's much like a road map. There may be detours ahead, but if you don't know where you're going, it's hard to find the best route.

Not everyone is a school psychologist or case manager, though, right? But you aren't without necessary skills. Once I had that framework to use—one that I knew well and was familiar with—then I began taking charge. I could use my competencies as well as my love and devotion to help my parents while also raising my children. But even if you're not a case manager or school psychologist you can do this. Pull from what you know.

If you're a marketing person—structure a sales campaign.

If you're an architect—draw up a building plan and project plan.

If you're an attorney—build a case.

If you're on the PTA—use your event-planning skills.

Author? Write an outline.

Teacher? Lesson plan.

Volunteer at your house of worship? Structure a plan to raise money, get more volunteers, coordinate an outreach event.

Stay-at-home mom—well you're already a boss because you have to juggle everything by managing multiple schedules and household resources and interface with educational outlets like schools or homeschool agencies. In my experience, stay-at-home moms tend to have incredible management skills.

In almost every endeavor where we manage others or are working to earn a paycheck, we're in service of others. They are our "clients." We use our skills sets to get a job done to their specifications and help them meet their needs. Who are our clients now? Parents, children, partner, and self. In addition, it helps to compartmentalize so that your emotions don't drive every decision. My point is, part of this challenge is knowing how to leverage the skills you have, reframe the challenge so that you can apply and adapt your knowledge, pull in help where you need it, and thus continue to manage your mindset towards building a Legacy of Love.

## My Story

*I start with getting a good assessment. I seek out a Senior Care Agency in my area, Eskaton. My parents have a long-term health insurance plan that provides primarily for assisted living. But getting the insurance approved is a process that includes assessment. The policy will pay for an extensive assessment by a qualified agency. That makes it easy for me. Assessment! That's what I do as a school psychologist. I know and appreciate assessment. I also know I am only qualified to do certain assessments, and they're NOT senior-care related. But I know I can grasp how a full assessment might look and what information it might yield. I am on the right path.*

*A geriatric care manager and a geriatric nurse visit my parents in their home. The assessment takes about two hours and includes extensive interviews with my parents individually and together, inspection of their home and cars, and a long interview with me. I hadn't thought about looking at my parents' cars, but it makes sense once I follow the Care Manager through the garage. My mom is a bit over a year into her diagnosis of Alzheimer's disease. She tends to have problems with short-term memory, but she still drives her car.*

*In looking at my mom's car, the care manager asks about scratches and small dents. My mom can't really recall how any of them got there. She wasn't even aware there were so many. She is certain that other people must have hit her car, maybe in a parking lot. "Hmmm," I think. "Probably not, Mom!"*

*This is eye opening.*

*The nurse, for her part, discovers the pillbox fiasco I described earlier. She is quite concerned about not only the number and types of meds my dad is taking, but the added complication that my mom, with compromised short-term memory due to Alzheimer's, is "helping" him put his meds in his pillbox.*

*My dad has vascular dementia brought on by a stroke and several TIAs (Transient Ischemic Attack, often called mini-strokes) over the last ten years. We discuss having nursing support throughout the week, but long-term care insurance won't pay for that. Can we afford it as private pay? We need to look at the numbers.*

*Both the nurse and the care manager are concerned about fall* risks in the home and how much my dad is isolating himself. They are concerned about cooking and my mom's memory.

There are a lot of concerns.

I wonder, "Well, do these folks just want my parents to enter one of their very high-priced facilities? Is this a scam?" This is uncharted territory for me, and I am suspicious and uncomfortable.

But after looking over their findings and reflecting on the questions they asked me, their recommendations for a move to an assisted living facility or daily in-home care feels well founded. They don't push any facility, and they actually offer to help me find a variety of places to tour.

The nurse and case manager both ask my parents about what they envision in their future. They ask me as well. My parents are not eager to move. They love their home. It is their dream retirement home. They have a lot of friends, community, and comforts. But it is also clear that they are unaware of how much they have declined over the last three years. They socialize less. My mom has dropped out of most volunteer activities and she has "forgotten" to read the books from her book club. In fact, she has missed several months of book club meetings. She can't recall the last book she read or the last meeting she attended. One night at church, I ask one of her friends from the book club about mom's attendance. Mom has not been to a meeting in a long time.

In fact, following this assessment, a neighbor of my parents calls to tell me she is worried about my them but doesn't want to interfere. She knows they have missed some garbage days, and she now calls them weekly to see if they need help putting out the cans.

I glimpse the looming sunset.

## Applying the Concepts of Case Management

The assessment data from the senior care agency and some anecdotal data from friends helped me get a better picture of what was really happening. As a result, I felt more confident that I could work with my parents to develop a plan. I also knew more critical conversations were on the horizon, and daunting tasks lay ahead. I needed to gather the support of my siblings and my husband to help my parents make some changes.

The assessment, neighbor's insight, my gut feelings, and my experience as a case manager all came together. I had to use my knowledge and experience to create a "plan" for my parents. I did a comparison in my head. I envisioned transferring concepts of an IEP to a plan for my parents as something like this:

| PARENT PLAN | |
|---|---|
| **Strengths** | Likes social activities such as card games |
| **Needs** (based on assessment) | Safe opportunities to socialize and exercise |
| **Goals** | Increase opportunities for social interaction and exercise |
| | Service Provider Responsible: Adult Day Care Center |
| | How will this be measured/ evaluated? Time spent weekly in activities |
| | Timeline for monitoring: Monthly |

I repeat: Assessment is key. A clear sense about current levels of functioning is critical. You might think of this as client needs or client pain points that you need to address. From there, considering the conversations about what an aging parent wants for the end of their life, it's much easier to form a plan of action. It beats haphazardly taking a stab at this or that and "spitting in the wind." A plan provides direction.

## The Value of Unbiased Assessment

Can you do this sort of assessment yourself? Yes, but keep in mind it's hard to be unbiased. I highly recommend enlisting a professional, such as a geriatric case manager or geriatric nurse. Family members might work, or if that is not advisable, ask a trusted friend for help. It's helpful to have a professional or neutral party to help you review information. This is a good question for the primary care doctor. Does insurance or the healthcare plan cover such an assessment? Can some of this be done in the doctor's office? Having a professional is best, but a trusted friend who can tell you that you might be overlooking this or that can take the anxiety out of the process.

A neutral person who is skilled in this area and is unbiased also eases your conversations with your parents about making changes in their lives. My parents took things more seriously from their physician or from the senior care team that evaluated them in their home than they would from me. It's not that they didn't trust me, but I had a different role with them. Also, I'd begun to make that shift in the change in our relationship, but they hadn't. They were still my parents, and it was hard for them to admit vulnerabilities to me. Having someone else talk with them was valuable.

If your parents don't easily trust outside professionals, it can still be helpful to have a non-family member with you when you talk to them about significant potential changes, such as getting help in the home or moving to a new living situation. While it was important for me to compartmentalize to figure out what I needed to do, in the presence of my parents I needed the safe space of interacting with them from my heart. Having another person there to sometimes say the hard stuff was good for me and productive for my parents.

# What are the signs a parents might need more help?

Difficulty with Activities of Daily Living (often referred to as ADLs) is specifically what doctors and professionals in senior services look for to determine if a person needs more care. This is, in part, what most insurance companies will look for to trigger paying for in-home care, assisted living or some types of senior services. This is not a comprehensive list. A professional skilled in this area will be needed to conduct this type of evaluation. But these are areas for you to start noticing, if you haven't already. Are there big changes here? Do you have concerns? Start taking notes if you can.

- Cooking

- Bathing

- Home maintenance and cleaning

- Running errands

- Frequent Falls

- Driving difficulty

  o Look for dings on the car

  o Traffic violations

  o Limiting driving – if this is unusual

- Social Isolation

- Forgetfulness

- Missed appointments

- Getting lost

- Trouble recalling routines

- Not taking medications properly

- Emergency room visits or increase in frequency

- Money management issues – if this is out of the ordinary
  o Missed bills

A professional case manager or a care team will likely develop a plan like the one I envisioned. Be sure to get a copy of any plan they develop. Make sure you are comfortable with the direction and the goals. Even though most of us can't take on the role of a geriatric case manager at the drop of a hat, we can consider what we know is best for our parents, what meets their stated desires and needs, and begin to be a strong advocate for their new normal.

# Transition

We are approaching a new normal, and that is challenging to the human goal of seeking a status quo. Human beings resist change. We are built to seek homeostasis—keep the organism running the same way, keep the patterns, keep the routines. But change is always happening, and big changes in our lives mean transitioning from one stage to another. If COVID has taught us anything, it is that!

The real irony is that as a Sandwich Generation person, people in transition surround us!

Our children are growing up, and that brings a whole host of changes. If you've lived through infant to toddler, toddler to school age, school age to tween, tween to teen, teen to young adult, then you know! Curiously, we often forget our own transitions in those ages and stages, but if we are honest with ourselves, we can recall the delight and pains in growing up. In addition, even though we aren't changing at light speed like our kids, we're changing every day in response to all the challenges and growth opportunities that confront us.

The stage we don't have firsthand experience with yet is the stage our parents currently face. This makes it hard for us to fully connect with our compassion and empathy. We can identify with the pain of our first heartbreak as a teen, but can we fully empathize with losing the ability to balance our checkbook or losing our friends one by one as they age and pass away? We likely can't recall being an infant and having a wet diaper, so can we imagine how hard it is to need one again? Or to need help changing it?

One of the unique challenges of the Sandwich Generation is being caught between two different developmental stages with our loved ones. Our lives, too, are now in transition. Perhaps we had an image of how our life would be. We would raise our kids, do the usual things, meet their teachers, deal with homework, go to little league games, ride bikes together, take a trip to Disneyland or Six Flags, swim in a lake or river or ocean or community pool. We anticipated fighting with our teenager, cringing when they learn to drive; we recall crying buckets when they graduated from kindergarten, sighed with relief when they were promoted from eighth grade, praised God when they graduated from high school. But in this dream, we probably didn't imagine our parents needing us so intimately, so deeply, so early. They were supposed to be the grandparents who helped us. And maybe they did. Maybe part of the transition and loss is loss of our support system.

My parents were a tremendous help to my family. They were the best babysitters. They were cheerleaders, showing up to soccer games, swim meets, and First Communions. They doted and spoiled when my husband and I were scraping by. My mom was my surrogate room mother at my kids' elementary school, since I worked full time. As a former teacher, she was delighted to chaperone field trips or to help out in a classroom. My dad enjoyed teaching my son the finer aspects of golf, his own lifelong passion. They occasionally took the kids for a weekend so we could enjoy some couple time. It was fantastic. They loved it and so did we. It was hard to watch that slip away. I was lucky that by the time they started to need more than they could give, my kids were older and not in need of babysitters. My kids became helpers for them. That wasn't so bad, either.

But all of this isn't necessarily what we envisioned. And that's where the difficulty in transition comes into play.

Transitions are not easy for everyone. Transitions occur in stages. In fact, they often put us in reverse, because they start with an ending of some sort. I learned that from reading the work of William Bridges.[3] He observed that a change is not just something being different or an added task or responsibility. It starts with a loss. If we get more heaped on our plate, then we lose time and peace of mind. If we now must do more for our parents, then it's likely they are not doing as much for us anymore. Another loss.

This may sound selfish, but it's normal for us to see big changes as losses. We lose what we know, what was familiar, and we have to learn a new routine, a new job, and a new normal.

After something familiar ends, we often hang out in a period of confusion until we can fully embrace or accept the new situation. This time period, which Bridges called the Neutral Zone, can be quick or last for a long time. We are processing our feelings, trying out new routines, learning new rhythms. We fail a lot in this confusing time. It makes me think of circus performers spinning plates on long poles, running in circles, trying to keep all the plates in the air, adding new plates here and there. Finally, there are too many plates and they begin to crash to the ground. Or a juggler, starting with three balls. Someone tosses another ball into the mix, then a bowling ball or a chainsaw. This is gonna hurt!

Eventually, we get through it. We manage to learn some new tricks. We may have some broken plates or a few nicks and cuts from the chainsaws, but we learn our new job. We have a new beginning.

The hardest part of transitions is being aware that we are in one, learning to be gentle with ourselves, and honoring the process. But we can do it. The first step is to acknowledge that it's a process, that this new era is part of our journey toward a sunset. How we show up for this sunset is a vital part of building a Legacy of Love.

# "There is no cure for aging."

# 6

# RUTHLESS SELF-CARE

*Love yourself first, and everything else falls into line.*
*You really have to love yourself to get anything done in*
*this world.*

Lucille Ball

As a parent and a psychologist, I am amazed at what great lengths people will go to protect and care for their children. I have amazed myself by muscling through a headache and still getting dinner on the table, giving the kids a bath, and reading stories before bed. It had to be done, so I did it.

## My Story

*Several times I have jumped in to fight for my children or support them, such as questioning our family physician when something didn't seem right with our son. We had elected to work with a family practice rather than one doctor for us and a different doctor for our son. However, at about 15 months old, he started getting frequent ear infections. Allergies, the physician said. I took him off milk and gave him soy. He went through several rounds of antibiotics. We used a humidifier and bought hypoallergenic mattress covers and sheets and a HEPA air filter. But the ear infections continued. More and more rounds of antibiotics seemed harmful to me, but the doctor felt that was the best course. I asked friends and co-workers about pediatricians in our area.*

*We consulted a pediatrician who referred us to an ear, nose and throat (ENT) doctor. At about age two, our son was still babbling incoherently and saying no real words. A speech pathologist diagnosed him with expressive and receptive language delays. The results of an audiological exam were scary—potential hearing loss. The ENT recommended ear tubes. He suggested that continuing antibiotics would likely not fix the problem and could possibly cause more health issues. The pediatrician concurred. While we were terrified of invasive surgery, we knew we had to do something, so we agreed. When the ENT came out of surgery, he told us it was great that we agreed to ear tubes, because it looked like glue behind his ear drums. If ear tubes didn't fix the problem, we would likely be talking about hearing aids. Our son responded almost immediately to speech therapy, and his improved hearing made a significant difference in so many parts of his life. He slept better, he could regulate his behavior more readily, and he could finally communicate effectively. I wasn't a doctor and wasn't qualified to figure this problem out myself, so I had to advocate and push. It paid off.*

*Parents do what needs to be done.*

I have many other examples, and you likely have your own. I've met parents of children with special needs who are fierce advocates for their children, and rightly so, as changes need to happen for people who have special needs. I think of the battles my mother waged in my defense when I was a child. I was diagnosed with Juvenile Rheumatoid Arthritis (JRA) at age six, and in the late 1960s few treatment options were available. I was lucky that my parents found a pioneering physician who developed a treatment center for such childhood diseases. The treatment for my illness was primarily no weight-bearing activity. I didn't attend school for the full year as a kindergartner or as a first grader. Until I was about 13, I was either in a wheelchair at school and medically excused from physical education, or I was at home on bed rest. My parents waged a number of battles on my behalf, since special education was not yet the law of the land. They persuaded my schools to provide a wheelchair for me, and teachers made accommodations for different aspects of in-class work and homework levels when I was out for doctor appointments or too fatigued to attend class or complete loads of homework.

Bottom line: My mother and father went up against the school system to make sure my needs were met. They fought. They advocated. They pushed buttons. They did what they felt they had to do, no matter what.

Fighting for someone you love feels like part of the job, part of the plan, part of the role.

Parents—especially mothers—often put others before themselves and end up exhausted. But in the big picture, it's essential to care for ourselves as fiercely as we do for our children or for those we love.

We can't drive anywhere on an empty gas tank. Similarly, we cannot pour water from an empty vessel. As they say on every flight, "Put your own oxygen mask on first."

The truth: When you're caring for others, self-care is essential. For many people, it feels selfish to put themselves first. But self-care is not synonymous with being self-centered or self-indulgent. It doesn't mean you must constantly treat yourself with scented candles, a glass of wine as you sink into a bubble bath, or a masseuse or a personal chef—although any of these activities can help relieve stress.

The self-care I'm talking about is self-compassion, and it's the opposite of pampering, selfishness, or self-centeredness. It's recognizing you are already EMPOWERED.

In fact, it's selfish not to care for ourselves; when we don't, we can't serve others. As parents, we must learn how to keep ourselves going so we're there for our kids. In the Sandwich Generation we must care for ourselves, so we can care for our children and our parents. Our self-care is an incredible gift for our children—they learn the value of loving themselves.

There's no better way to build a Legacy of Love than by loving ourselves.

## The Elements of Self-Care

I wish I could've afforded a weekly massage, a chauffeur, a daily chef, and a personal trainer. But I couldn't.

What I could afford was to visit a doctor yearly and as needed. I could take a day of sick leave when I was ill, so I could recover more quickly. I could challenge myself to ask for help when I needed it, and that was the hardest of all. These all sound simple, but I know that for many they are a privilege. Many Sandwich Generation parents might not have paid sick leave—certainly not stay-at-home parents or those working part-time.

I didn't always take good care of myself, but I learned over time that I needed to take as much time and energy to care for myself before I willingly and sometimes *resentfully* gave everything I had to others. That meant setting boundaries, checking in with myself, and staying healthy.

I've learned that self-care is as much a practice of mindset as it is about specific activities or interventions.

Am I worth it? Do I value myself? Can I fight for my needs? Can I ask for help without feeling like a burden?

Can I wrap my head around the notion that "it's better to give than to receive" does not mean running myself into the ground?

In fact, if I don't take care of myself, then I can't give.

That's selfish.

I had to work on those concepts a lot, and to be honest, I still do.

Taking a year off from work to research and write this book about the Sandwich Generation—something I really wanted to do in order to serve others—was a big step for me. It wasn't an ideal time.

Our son was beginning his senior year of college, and our daughter (our youngest child) was just starting her freshman year. Both attended private universities. We'd saved money for college, and we both worked and did fairly well. My husband was a successful entrepreneur, so I was the one with the steady job that came with healthcare benefits. If I were to take a year off, we would need to pay out of pocket for health insurance.

We crunched the numbers. They didn't look great, but it seemed doable, especially if I could pick up some money on the side as a life coach and Licensed Educational Psychologist (LEP), which I very much wanted to do. My husband's job was flourishing, and he was getting more and more work and offers for collaborative projects and speaking engagements.

We took the plunge.

For the first few months, we enjoyed playing a bit, and I travelled with my husband when his work took him to fun places like Italy and Australia. This gave us time together before we headed into our next phase of parenting—that of intermittent empty nesters with kids living away at college part of the year.

But by late December, we became frantic, realizing that the lack of my salary, the cost of healthcare, and the burden of two college tuitions were more costly than the numbers had looked when I negotiated my sabbatical.

I had to deal with my guilt over taking time for myself. How indulgent, I thought. "C'mon Christy!" I scolded myself. "Who do you think you are?"

I fought through feelings of indulgence, as if somehow I hadn't really earned this time. I thought my "value" was in my salary and the benefits.

I told myself all the things most caregivers and many women do. I am not my dreams; I am what I can give or do.

At one point, when both were home for Christmas, I told my kids more specifically what I was doing and writing. Both encouraged me. They told me how important they thought a book like this would be. They told me they were proud of me. And I took some time to let that sink in. I took time to realize I was still a parent and that this was an opportunity for me to model self-care. Part of that was believing in my dreams. They watched when my husband started his own business and his dreams took off, and now it was my time to do that.

I gave them a gift by facing my fears and moving forward. Delving more deeply into writing, which had always been a passion but one I rarely pursued officially, hinted to them how life-giving following dreams can be. I wanted living authentically despite the challenges, learning new things at any age, and being true to self to be part of my Legacy of Love for them.

Taking the time off also freed me to do some caregiving for a couple of dear friends with significant health crises. I hadn't been able to do that before. It was a gift to me to be able to help. One was adjusting to a new normal of dialysis, and the other faced the first weeks of radiation and chemotherapy. These caregiving stints were my choice—my choice to give back to dear friends who had seen me through tough times not long ago when my parents were dying. Both had lost their parents before I did, and I leaned on them for advice and cried on their shoulders more than once. Now, I could be there for them.

Getting better and better at setting limits and practicing self-care gave me energy and opportunity to give in ways I couldn't have previously. I had more space in my mind and more ability to be present not only to the needs of others, but more importantly, to myself.

## Steps of Self-Care

Say out loud to yourself:

- "I deserve to take care of myself."

- "I am worth my time."

- "I have the right and responsibility to say 'No,' set limits, and ask for help."

How does it feel to say these statements out loud?

Does it feel true? Can you live with that? Can you stand in a space and feel that down to your bones?

For most givers this is challenging. But with practice, we can start to take baby steps to do one thing daily to increase our well-being.

It's like dental hygiene. We brush our teeth every morning and every evening. Practicing self-care is equally important. It's mental hygiene.

Dental hygiene. Mental hygiene.

Dental health. Mental health.

I developed a self-care workshop for caregivers. I focused on the mindset of self-care first. Then, borrowing from Special Education, I introduced the concept of an Individual Energy Plan—personal IEP. (I had seen something similar at a conference and loved the concept.) It's a model, a process, and it might just work for you, too. Part of what I developed includes a self-care assessment and a format for the Individual Energy Plan for my coaching practice. It's a work in progress and ever evolving, as are we.

## Step One: Assessment

For caregivers (or anyone really) it's important to first do a self-assessment. What are your needs? What's falling off your plate? You can find examples of caregiver self-assessments online or use the one from Chapter 3, which is also located in the Resources section at the back of this book.

## Step Two: Identify Barriers

What do you imagine gets in the way of putting yourself first?

- **Money.** Do you imagine you will need to spend a lot of money and it's already tight?

- **Time.** Do you imagine you will need to take precious time away from children, partner, and your parents?

- **Knowledge.** Do you imagine you don't know any self-care routines? Are you spending a lot of time researching what to do with your parents?

- **People.** Are there folks who stress you out or drain you more than others? Who are the people who fill you up, encourage, and support you?

- *Physical.* Are you physically worn out? Do you, yourself, require a doctor visit? Are there interventions you can take on that do not require a prescription?

## Step Three: Identify Assets

Who's in your corner? What other resources or services can you leverage to help you with tasks and time?

If you work outside the home, consider taking advantage of an Employee Assistance Program. It can provide up to ten sessions of counseling or therapy to help you develop strong coping strategies.

Investigate your health provider system. Many offer free or low-cost educational workshops to help people reduce stress or learn new habits.

Specifically look at the following:

**People:** Spouse, children, friends, neighbors, colleagues at work, friends from a faith group, or others from groups you are active in such as PTA, church, community groups.

It may feel awkward to ask some of these folks to help, but people want to contribute. People have a need to help others. How many times have you stepped in to help someone—a list goes around for meal sign-ups for someone battling cancer or has lost a loved one. We jump in. Others will jump in for you, too.

**Service Providers**: Paid resources abound as well, such as geriatric case managers, caregivers, and in-home support services. With many in-home support services, you can hire help for one day a week. That may not seem like a lot, but if you're doing everything, one day a week feels like a trip to the Bahamas. Some insurance policies cover this type of care.

What about hiring someone to come into your home for your needs? You might be able to hire a dog walker, housecleaner, or cook. A teen or college student might jump at the chance for occasional work if you plant the seed. Put the word out, and people will contact you. Be sure to check out resources in order to feel comfortable and safe, but if it's doable, try it. For personal service, ask for references or look for testimonials on websites. If it's a place, such as a spa or yoga studio, find online reviews and check out their websites.

## Step Four: Your Self-Care Goals

Develop SMART Goals for yourself. SMART goals are: specific, measurable, attainable, relevant, and time specific. Don't attempt to change everything at once. One goal at a time is enough to start, and other changes will fall into place. Consider a change in your morning and a change in your evening, maybe a form of exercise. Never underestimate the value of exercise. Research touting the benefits of walking 30 minutes per day abounds. Taking 30 minutes for yourself might sound difficult, but the benefits will quickly become apparent in the reduction of stress.

An example of a SMART goal is: ***I will walk for 30 minutes 4 days a week in order to reduce stress for a period of 3 months.*** This is a goal that is specific, measurable, attainable, relevant, and time specific.

## Step Five: Monitor

Figure out a way to monitor your goal to determine if it is working for you or if it needs some modification. A simple checklist will do. Don't make this complicated! Literally, just make a tick mark on a paper calendar each day you exercise, or stick a Post-It note on your bathroom mirror each week and tick off each day you exercise. Use an app on your phone. Do whatever works for you.

## Step Six: Accountability

Find someone to share your goal or goals with. Not only will this help you to stay focused on meeting your goal, but it also gives you an added layer of support. Getting this kind of support will make it easier to ask for and receive other types of support. Find a friend, co-worker, or neighbor who has similar struggles, so that you can share the load.

# Step Seven: Celebrate

Stop and appreciate success! Making changes is tough, and we don't like it. So, acknowledge how far you've come.

An Individual Energy Plan may be too much for some people. It's highly structured, and it can provide a great deal of support. But if it feels like too much, DON'T DO IT! This is self-care, remember? Do what works.

Here are some FREE and easy self-care habits that yield great results. Each one is healthy and doable. They don't require an Individualized Energy Plan or a coach. Maybe you are already doing some of these; if so, take time to congratulate yourself.

- **Sleep.** Seven to eight hours for most adults. Sleep is best in a cool, dark room. A humidifier or a low, white-noise maker can help. Multiple digital sleep apps are available, many of them free.

- **Clean eating.** The food you put in your body makes a difference. Buy more food that rots within a few days, because then you know it's fresh. Stuff that lasts on our pantry shelf for years doesn't help our bodies. Clean eating promotes a healthy gut, as well. A growing body of research indicates that our gut health impacts our brains and overall bodily functions.

- **Hydration.** Clean water. Limit caffeine and alcohol. Limiting is not the same as abstaining. If your lifestyle includes caffeine and alcohol, so be it. But limiting both is wise. I do not consume more than one cup of coffee in a day and never after noon in order to promote good sleep at night.

- **Hugs.** Just for the health of it!! (And, I always add, with permission.) Healthy physical contact with others releases feel-good hormones such as oxytocin. Good for you, good for them. In this time, your spouse or partner, kids, and parents may need a few extra hugs, and you most certainly will.

- **Exercise.** Thirty minutes of walking a day can change your life! If walking isn't fun, turn on an exercise video or dance to your favorite tunes. You do not need a gym membership, but a little sweat every day is important. If you are physically caring for your parents or children, I also recommend stretching before any physical caregiving.

- **Good skin care.** Not expensive products, but do clean and moisturize daily. Skin is the largest organ of our body, and we need to pay attention to it. Hydration helps, both inside and out. So that harkens back to the drink-water note above.

- **Find your people!** Do you need support? There's a group for that! Check your faith-based organizations for grief, marriage support, and other groups. I have enjoyed learning new things and meeting new and interesting people through online Meetup groups. Google Meetup and find a group that appeals to you. Most are free.

- **Be aware of how you feed your soul and brain.** What are you watching on TV or online? What are you listening to? If watching the news or listening to horrifying stories creates anxiety, then stop it! You can still be well informed. But feeling enraged or frightened for extended periods of time increases stress and anxiety.

- **Practice mind-body techniques.** Consider meditation or Emotional Freedom Techniques (EFT or tapping,) yoga, tai chi. Numerous mind-body techniques are easy to follow and free. Take a class through our local parks and recreation center or from a private studio. There are also a gazillion supportive YouTube videos and apps. Try out a few until you find one or more that work.

- **Finally, GRATITUDE.** A growing body of research identifies the simple strategy of writing a daily gratitude list as one of the best ways to reduce stress and increase resilience. In fact, if you Google "research on gratitude practice," you'll find nearly 50 million results. Amazon carries nearly 50,000 gratitude journal options. Studies on gratitude suggest that being thankful is highly correlated to lower rates of depression, anxiety, and other mental health conditions and highly predictive of higher levels of well-being.

## Role Model Self-Care

When you begin to take care of yourself in earnest, you'll feel the effects, if not immediately, then certainly sooner than you might think. There will be times when you feel rushed and you think you can't take five minutes for yourself. *Resist that.* There will be times when others complain that you are taking time for yourself. *Ignore them.* There will be times when someone asks, "What about me?" And this is when you can say, *"I am doing this **for** you."*

Our children are always watching us. That's why taking care of yourself is so important. Encourage your children to find new or additional ways to care for themselves. By watching you, learning from you, your children will find more ways to adapt to the challenges that they will inevitably encounter. You are a role model every time you make time for yourself—or don't. Resilience is a learned skill. Growing up with a resilient parent—not one who tries to hide behind the façade of perfection—is great for children. They see that you can make it through tough times, and when their tough times come, they will know that they can make it through.

## The Trifecta

One other aspect seemingly intertwined with the Sandwich Generation is that, for women, it often coincides with a delicate and challenging time—the era of menopause.

Just a short personal rant here, but seriously, when I get into the car, I inevitably hear a commercial for erectile dysfunction (ED) medication. I see ads for ED meds in major magazines and newspapers. But I never hear about menopause, and unless a woman had her ovaries surgically removed before the onset of puberty, every woman who lives past a certain point will experience menopause. It's not often talked about, and it's generally different for each woman. Typically, women experience menopause between the ages of 40 and 60; age 51 is currently the median age in the U.S. This just happens to be the timeframe that many women are in the Sandwich Generation.

Teens, Parents, Menopause, or Win! Place! Show! You won the Trifecta!

I honestly did not pay attention to my body as much as I could have during menopause. Brain fog, weight gain, irritability, insomnia, even missed periods—I chalked these up to stress and anxiety. I visited the doctor as needed, but we didn't talk much about menopause. Sadly, I couldn't talk to my mother about it, either. Even in the early stages of Alzheimer's, she wasn't fully able to have a deep-dive discussion about her journey through menopause. Her information on health issues or any issues of substance was not reliable; she was just too fuzzy. She'd had breast cancer just after menopause, though, and she had voiced strong opinions about hormone therapy years ago, but she couldn't recall what she took, when she took it, or anything about her outcomes. I'd been too young and preoccupied to take notes back then.

Frankly, our society doesn't talk much about menopause. Menopausal women are often portrayed as the butt of the joke. How many cartoons have you seen that make fun of the woman having hot flashes? So, it's no surprise that I didn't connect the dots, but looking back, I wish I had.

As I said at the outset, this is the book I wish I'd had. Talk to your doctor about menopause whenever you feel it's time to do so—in fact, earlier. Talk to your mother if you can. Information about your biological mother's experience is useful, but an adoptive mother or aunt can also shed some light on this inevitable part of your life as a woman. Talk with other women who are willing to share and learn along with you.

Menopause is a major part of women's lives, and it impacts our family members too. The life change is huge; I'm amazed we don't give it more attention. That it often coincides with Sandwich Generation chaos sort of fits the pattern: a big life change we can't accurately put on the calendar, it doesn't get a lot of media attention, and yet it shapes our personal lives and the lives of our children.

## Medication and Therapy

While I didn't connect the dots to realize I was in the midst of menopause, I did talk to my doctor about anti-anxiety medication. I told her what was going on at home, that I was working full time and raising kids and now managing the care of my parents. I was a wreck! She suggested anti-anxiety medication as a way to take the "edge" off. I didn't want sleep medication, but finding a way to reduce anxiety, even if just a little, sounded marvelous. I agreed, and it helped a lot. After a few weeks, I was less in reaction mode and better able to ride the waves of stress. I snapped less at my kids, my husband, and my parents. I felt less "clenched." My teeth weren't clenched, my fists relaxed, and what I noticed most is that my shoulders were no longer located just below my earlobes! I was able to relax my neck and shoulders.

I also sought out a therapist. I took advantage of the Employee Assistance Program at my workplace and found a woman I liked. We worked together for the allotted ten sessions, but I wanted more. She was willing to continue and gave me a good rate, thank goodness. It helped to have a place to let it all out, to explore my mixed feelings and changing relationships with my parents, siblings, children, and myself.

A year after my parents died, I slowly went off of the medication. I replaced it with better, more enhanced self-care strategies, because I had the time and space to do so. My emotional bandwidth had been restored, and I found I was able to manage just fine. I'm glad to be off of anti-anxiety medication now, but I am glad I was willing and able to use it under the care of a physician in a healthy manner.

I eventually let therapy go, too. With my background in counseling, psychology, and mental health, I fully support working with a therapist. But at some point our relationship shifted, and I no longer needed to dig through the past or present with a therapist. Eventually, however, I desired to work with a coach. While therapy often looks back or looks at what's not right at the moment, coaching is future focused. I wanted someone to help me in areas where I didn't have expertise, such as writing a book, developing content in an online business, developing a private practice as a Licensed Educational Psychologist or as a life coach.

I've had incredible mentors in my life, some who were dear friends or supervisors. I've also benefitted from working with mental health professionals and coaches. Sometimes I need to get out of my own way, and skilled professionals have been instrumental in keeping me moving forward. I share this openly with my children.

It's another way I am trying to build the Legacy of Love.

## " *There's no better way to build a Legacy of Love than by loving ourselves.* "

# 7

# THE ROLE OF FAITH, SPIRIT, NATURE, OR UNIVERSE

*I believe in evolution. But I also believe, when I hike the Grand Canyon and see it at sunset, that the hand of God is there also.*

**John McCain**

Today people talk a great deal about spirituality. For some that means religion or a faith tradition. For some it's a synonym for God, nature, spirit, or universe. Whether religious, spiritual, agnostic, or atheist, people generally have some idea of how things come to be, what other power or understanding is creating life or participating in life. It's not surprising that in times of struggle people think more about this.

Spirituality and religion are a great comfort for some people. Now might be a good time to consider how to integrate your parents' beliefs into their care. Faith traditions and spiritual traditions or some other understanding are likely to impact how your parents view death. It's not unusual for people to become more focused on these beliefs as they age. Studies by psychologists and others in the medical field point to the role of spirituality in health and end of life. There is abundant evidence that spirituality provides increased levels of comfort in those who are facing death. Numerous studies point to spirituality or religious beliefs promoting longevity. Hospice agencies provide a support person to help families pull these spiritual resources together. Most religious communities offer end-of-life support and send priests, clerics, pastors, and other leaders to visit those who are dying. That support is also meant for the family and caregivers.

Here are some questions to consider:

- What do you do if you are not particularly spiritual but your parents are?

- What if your parents' faith is different from your own?

- What if you suspect a parent is being harmed—for instance, being asked for frequent donations or large sums of money for cures or prayers or some other engagement?

For most people I have heard from on the issue of spirituality, it comes down to honoring your parents' wishes. Given that beliefs are foundational for many people, especially at the end of life, it's an essential part of health care. This is a good reason to discuss what a parent wants to include for their care.

Understanding your parents' weekly or daily spiritual practice can help you work with their care team, doctors, and other providers. Get a full understanding of what role spirituality plays in their life, so that you can adequately and responsibly share it with the team. Whether your parent is in the hospital, a skilled nursing or assisted living facility, in their own home or yours, there are ways to ensure that they receive the ongoing benefits and comfort that spirituality and religion can bring to them. Most places of worship have outreach services to homebound or ill members. Connect with the people in these programs to find out how they can continue to support your parent. If your parent isn't affiliated with a place of worship, but in talking with them you realize that might be comforting, then reach out.

I've interviewed a number of people on this topic, and most are adamant that it's important to honor parents' faith wishes and practices. You can drive a parent to church, attend services with them, or find another ride for them to their place of worship, even if the ride is from someone who does not share their faith.

For me, it was no-brainer.

# My Story

*When my dad fell and broke a hip the last year of his life, we weren't sure he would pull through. He would need surgery—a huge risk for him due to his compromised cardiovascular system. The anesthesiologist was fairly blunt with me about his chances.*

*I called the Catholic Church where he and my mom had been founding members. Even though my parents no longer lived in the vicinity of the parish, I reached out to them rather than to the nearest Catholic Church.*

*I asked for a priest to come and pray with my dad, give him communion, or even administer the Sacrament of Anointing of the Sick, generally a sacrament given to those near death if deemed necessary. I thought it might be.*

*I believed this would provide a great deal of comfort for my dad. At the time, I didn't realize how much comfort it would be for me. After the priest visited, I was in tears in my husband's arms just outside my dad's room. It was heart rending.*

*But my father pulled through. I was so grateful I had asked for a priest, and I know it gave my father spiritual strength. It gave me spiritual strength as well.*

*About three months after my dad's hip surgery, he was nearing the end of his life. He had rallied some and was able to engage in some therapy, but after a bout of pneumonia and a couple of trips to the* emergency room, he was failing. The last time I had him in the ER, the physicians spoke to me about hospice. After consulting with family members by phone, I knew this was the right choice. I signed the papers and took him home.

That was a Monday night. My husband and I had been on a business trip abroad the week before. My sister and brother took some vacation time to come and visit with my parents. When we touched down on Sunday night, I retrieved my phone messages, several from family staying with my kids, alerting me that there had been some emergency room visits with both Mom and Dad. A friend had also called to say that a dear mutual friend of ours had quite recently and unexpectedly passed away.

Not great news after nearly ten hours of air travel.

On Monday morning, I visited my parents and immediately took my dad back to the ER. It was at the end of this day we started him with hospice.

By Friday of that week, my dad had slipped into unconsciousness. My mom was confused. She was using an oxygen tank for her own breathing problems; what was suspected to be pneumonia turned out to be a pleural effusion. She didn't really know what was going on with my dad. The staff at the assisted living facility had kept her involved in her normal daily routine while attending to my dad. They didn't want to tell her that he was dying until nearer to the end, so she could say her goodbyes. They needed her to be occupied so that they could focus on him, allowing him the peace and quiet he needed to pass. They were far more experienced than I in working with someone who had Alzheimer's, so I heeded their advice.

While my husband and children spent time with my mother, I contacted the parish once again to ask for a priest. We were far away from the parish, and I probably should have called a closer Catholic Church, but I was hoping I could get a priest who knew my family. I was so grateful that they sent the Parochial Vicar (assistant pastor priest) over to deliver the Sacrament of Anointing of the Sick now for *the second time.*

*Seven weeks later, to the day, Father Lawrence was summoned to administer the Sacrament of Anointing of the Sick to my mother. It was several weeks after my father died that we learned my mother's breathing difficulty was, in fact, the return of cancer, and it was likely terminal. The lining around her lungs was filled with fluid, and tests indicated breast cancer cells in the fluid. My mother had had a mastectomy nearly 20 years prior. Knowing my mom was near the end, I called my sister and brother. My sister had been there the week before and was not able to leave her family again. It was hard for her, but she had said her goodbyes and felt at peace. When my brother came, he brought his oldest son, my parents' first grandchild. She knew she knew him but had forgotten his name. He was a loving sport about it.*

*When the priest came, my brother, my nephew, my daughter, and I were all gathered around my mom. My daughter, who was very close to my mom, sat at her feet and held her hand. She smiled up into her eyes, talked with her, and gently, lovingly answered the same questions again and again as if my mom had asked them for the first time. I could barely contain my tears to witness this incredible act of love. My nephew, too, answered questions and never flinched when my mom could not remember what he had just said, his name, or that he had told her that he and his wife were expecting her first great-grandchild soon.*

*Father Lawrence asked us to gather and hold hands. He led us in saying the Lord's Prayer. He leaned over her and gently made a sign of the cross on her forehead with oil. Her eyes were closed, and she wore an almost beatific smile. I am not sure she was aware of receiving the Sacrament of the Anointing of the Sick, but she seemed so happy to have all of us there praying.*

*She died in her sleep the next morning. It was her 83rd birthday.*

*The time of sharing sunsets with my parents had come to a close. Having a faith practice gave me comfort through the shades of red, orange, purple, and blue.*

Studies suggest that nearly 66% of those who lose a spouse will die within the first three months after the spouse's death. It's called the Widowhood Effect. My mother was not well. She had Alzheimer's and now a recurrence of cancer. I was devastated that she died, but I have come to think she died of a broken heart and yearned to be with my dad, even though I know it was the cancer that killed her. I think of them as being out playing golf together at Pebble Beach or some other famous course, maybe even making a few holes in one. I think my dad must be ecstatic that he doesn't have to pay the exorbitant greens fees! These thoughts bring me comfort.

What I do know is that their spiritual beliefs held them up throughout their lives and made a huge difference in how they managed physical pain and how they transitioned into dying. I witnessed the comfort my dad received when he faced surgery, and I witnessed my mother's peace on her last night of life. My family was also lifted up through our spirituality. It's my belief in an afterlife that gives me peace and hope and comfort knowing my parents are together again.

Whether your family practices faith traditions or holds to some other form of spirituality, find ways to bring this into your care of your parents. Some spiritual or uplifting activities might be:

- Arranging times for family or friends to visit

- Making pilgrimages to meaningful places

- Looking through photos together

- Telling stories, even writing or recording histories

- Recalling events while going through memorabilia

What matters is that you take time to find out what is most important to your parents in the area of spirituality. Knowing this opens a door for dialogue and loving connection. However, it is important for this to be what your parents want and need. This might not be the time to debate or try to convince a parent of your faith and beliefs if they don't share them. That might really push some buttons for people who feel strongly about their own faith practice and the need to save someone from harm in an afterlife. So, if I tread on those beliefs, know that I err on the side of giving comfort to an aging parent.

**66** *Their spiritual beliefs made a huge difference in how that managed physical pain and how they transitioned into dying.* **99**

# 8

# THE SQUEEZE OF MONEY AND LEGAL ISSUES

*Many people take no care of their money till they come nearly to the end of it, and others do just the same with their time.*

**Johann Wolfgang von Goethe**

A book about the Sandwich Generation would not be complete without addressing money or legal issues. But be clear: I am not offering financial or legal advice.

Over the course of writing this book, I spoke to a number of people in the financial industry, and one told me that getting people to talk about their money was harder than getting them to talk about their sex life. Sounds about right! People seem to have mixed feelings like shame, guilt, and confusion about money and habits around money. But for people in the Sandwich Generation, money is always a concern. In fact, many of those in the middle of the Sandwich contribute substantial amounts of money to help support their aging parents. Going back to the 2013 Pew Research Center study, about one in four adults who assist their aging parents also contribute to their parents' overall financial picture. Of those contributing, about seven out of ten indicate they are contributing money consistently.

We in the Sandwich Generation are also providing care and contributions to our own children. I communicated with Jay Zagorsky, Ph.D., senior lecturer on markets, public policy, and law at Boston University's Questrom School of Business, about money issues with the Sandwich Generation. Briefly, he said that if he were addressing folks in the Sandwich Generation, he would ask that they look at the whole picture, not just at their parents, but how they are interacting with their children, too. In a 2012 paper published in the *Journal of Family and Economic Issues*, he used data from the National Longitudinal Survey of Youth 1979 to explore what happens to people who inherit wealth. He found roughly half spend the money or lose it in poor investments. I then asked him what he wanted to share with people in the Sandwich Generation, and this is what he offered:

A lot of people worry, "is there enough money" but this is only one important aspects of finances. Another important question is, can we protect what money is available?

As the person being sandwiched it is important to know that financial mistakes come in a U shaped pattern, with the number of mistakes on the Y axis and a person's age on the X. In simple terms this graph says.

1) Your kids don't know anything about money and are going tomess things up when they are young and learning.

2) You in the middle will not make too many mistakes.

3) However, your aging parents, who might have known a lot about handling their financial affairs a few decades ago, are now going to start making more mistakes as they age.

The U shaped pattern means you need to train both your kids and your parents financially. Kids need help to be able to successfully navigate the world of money on their own. (I am a believer in allowances and then having kids perform simple financial chores like buying food for dinner with a fixed budget, and then cooking it)

Parents need to understand that they are at risk for making poor financial decisions and also are more susceptible to fraud. Because of this they need to involve their middle age children more in their financial life and be less independent so that they don't make ruinous mistakes.

Money and legal concerns go hand in hand. These can be touchy subjects! I am not a financial professional or an attorney, so I can't offer financial or legal advice, but it's essential to get good advice regarding your parents' finances and legal concerns, as well as your own. Beyond that, when I reflect on my experiences and what I have learned from others, my thoughts on money and legal issues are not so much how to make money or maneuver through legal concerns or how to save money, but to consider our relationship to money, how we care for it legally, and how it influences our lives. As much of the research cited suggests, our money biases, our beliefs, and our bugaboos about legal affairs strongly impact our journey inside the Sandwich Generation.

## Your Parents' Money: Financial Matters

As I researched more deeply into financial matters for this book, I found a slew of financial professionals. Each has a different level of licensure. Different licensure means differing rates. Whether you are looking for a financial professional for yourself or your parents, do some due diligence. Take the time to investigate. You will save money and heartache and possibly keep family tempers in check.

What are financial professionals called? In short, a Financial Advisor is anyone who helps people manage their money. It's the umbrella term.

From there, you can find professionals who offer a variety of services and who have a variety of training and credentials. Some professionals will help with long-term money goals and growing your money, some will focus on debt repayment, some on insurance or tax planning. Keep in mind that your needs for an expert may differ from your parents' needs. There is no one-size-fits-all financial professional.

Ask friends or family members who may be in a similar situation for referrals for individual professionals or firms. Online matching services can assess your needs and direct you to several firms or professionals. Finding the right fit will provide welcome peace of mind.

## Estates and Trusts

I spoke to Stephan M. Brown, Esq., an estate attorney in Roseville, CA. Mr. Brown talked with me about several legal issues concerning aging adults and their families. He recommends establishing a Trust well before you are considered aging or elderly. Common triggers for establishing a Trust might be when a person or couple buys a house or has children. A Trust is designed to provide legal protection of a person's (Trustor's) assets and to ensure that in the event of their death, the assets are distributed according to their wishes. When assets are in Trust, it's possible to avoid Probate. Probate is a legal action by the state to authenticate a Last Will and Testament (what we commonly refer to as a Will), determine debts and assets, determine how debts will be paid, determine the rightful beneficiaries and how the remaining assets will be distributed to them. A Trust is greater protection than a Will in that it holds the assets in the Trust and avoids probate. It's not unusual for a Trust to also have a Pour-Over Will as a sort of "Plan B." A Pour-Over Will is a safeguard to make sure that any assets not identified in the Trust at the time of death will be "poured over" into the Trust, and thus also avoid probate.

As a trust and estate attorney, Mr. Brown has helped many families and individuals create these legal documents. He explains that in a Trust, the Trustor (the person or couple who are developing the Trust) will name the Trustees for the Trust. The Trustee or Trustees are people who will step in to manage the Trust when the Trustor is no longer able or at the time of his/her death, to help in the distribution of the assets. Trustees are obligated to act in the best interest of the Trust and the Trust's beneficiaries. Mr. Brown emphasizes the need to choose a reliable and willing person to be named as a Trustee. He suggests asking the person before naming them in the Trust.

Every Trust is different, according to Mr. Brown, and it's important for people to consider a number of things when developing one: Who are the beneficiaries; who will be a Trustee; what assets should be named in the Trust; what are contingency plans for minor children (should there be a plan for them to have their inheritance held in trust until the age of majority); and a number of other concerns. I asked if a person could develop a Trust on their own using online forms. Mr. Brown suggested that if one understands the legal process and has a very simple set of assets and a simple plan, then it might be okay, but he doesn't recommend it. A Trust provides substantial protection not only for the Trustor, but also for beneficiaries. In many cases, the beneficiaries are children, so it's important to take time to develop this with care, consideration, and clear-headedness.

The cost of developing a Trust will vary. At this writing, costs typically range from $1,000 to upwards of $2,500 or more, depending on the complexity of the Trust. There are also some minor differences from state to state, but in general, a Trust developed in one state is valid in another if a person or couple moves. But it's important to update it from time to time. In general, it's recommended that a Trust be updated every three years. The cost of this is far less than the original development.

Considering probate costs makes the decision easier. You may have heard horror stories about probate eating up all the assets or taking years, and in fact, probate can devour assets. Probate fees will be 4% of the first $100,000 and then additional percentages for each subsequent $100,000 on up to $1,000,000. If someone has a home, the probate charges will be based on the value of the home, not the equity in it. Designation or distribution of funds held in trust for a minor cannot be made until the child attains age 18. In addition, all the findings and distributions of the assets are public knowledge, since they are filed in public court. So, there are several reasons why taking time to establish a Trust is important, and it is a responsible and loving choice for a family. In terms of building a Legacy of Love, a Trust is right up there with some of our most compassionate acts.

I spoke with financial expert Carol Hunter, also known as "The Money Mender," who gave me tremendous insight. Carol primarily helps women to become financially independent and prosperous through her online and in-person coaching services. She shared that she often speaks to women about getting their estate in order for the future and helping parents get their affairs in order as well.

The biggest piece of advice she offered concerning aging is not only to draw up an estate plan, but also to work with a financial professional well versed in the pros and cons of different insurance products, someone who understands the Medicare and Social Security systems and how and when to apply for benefits and how those will impact long-term care in assisted living or aging in place in their home or yours. Every person's family is different, but finding someone skilled in these topics and licensed to give information is important.

Different professionals may have different opinions. I'm not giving legal or financial advice! However, I share these interviews so you that might start thinking about your own situation. I can't overstress the importance of professional advice. Licensed and trained financial and legal professionals are as critical as a licensed physician for medical needs. Yes, it's an expenditure of money, but it can save you in the long run.

**I stumbled upon another important angle in my research.** If your parent (or you) are in a same sex-marriage or partnership, the playing field is not level. Even if two people are legally married, some states continue to treat LGBTQ marriages and partnerships differently when it comes to legal matters and money. Finding a law firm that specializes in LGBTQ matters can be critical. Laws vary from state to state, so take special care to find a firm that can spell out what your parent or you might need.

## Why Estate Planning is Essential

For estate planning, consider enlisting the services of a trust or estate attorney. We often think we don't need to worry about estate planning unless we have, well, an ESTATE. But your estate is all your money in every form:

- Cash

- Bank accounts

- IRAs and 401K plans (or some variation, such as 403b)

- Stocks

- Bonds

- Insurance policies

- Annuities

- Real property, such as a house or condo or apartment

- Real estate, such as vacant land

- Cars

- Businesses, or a stake in a business or partnership

- Belongings

Most people have some kind of estate. It's not uncommon to

assume that things will simply be distributed, that family members will know who gets what, or that assets will be distributed evenly. That is not always the case. A written legal plan provides a framework for a person to:

- Manage assets while alive and well

- Plan and identify who will help manage assets when one can no longer reasonably do so

- Indicate clearly how assets should be distributed upon death

Attorneys who handle Trusts know that disagreements are not always obvious. Families can have disputes, and they can get ugly. People don't want to think about that. No one wants to think that their children will fight over assets. Even in the closest of families, there can be disagreements. One woman I interviewed described her family of five adult children as "very close." However, several years after their father had passed away and their mother was ailing, they scrambled to determine who would take care of mom. Disagreements arose, old, childhood resentments that made discussions challenging, at best.

This wasn't good for anyone. It required multiple conversations and negotiations and trial and error to reach consensus about who would take on the lion's share of duties. This family determined it was best to divide duties so that one person managed money while another managed healthcare. Power of Attorney documents were drawn up to designate who would do which task.

## My Story

*My siblings were grateful that I would take over. It made sense. My sister offered to manage the money remotely from Montana, but after looking at my parents' bills—what was paid online and what was not—and looking at their bookkeeping in general, I was not so sure this was the best idea.*

*My parents weren't particularly organized at that point, which was shocking, given how organized my father had always been. The little office in their home was piled with paper. They paid some bills online and others by check, but there was no rhyme or reason to that system. There were nearly 15 years' worth of bank statements, but some years were missing. There was every manner of printed material from their investment firm stacked in corners and against the wall. Most of this was obligatory mailing from different companies, but since my parents were not well versed in computers, they elected to get everything by mail.*

*Another reason for me to step in was proximity. While a lot can be done remotely, it would take a while to set that up, and even then there would be times when I knew I would have to step in to buy something or manage a situation involving money—like when they were ready to move, and it would be easier for me to have a debit card for their account.*

*In truth, I am not highly organized myself, especially when it comes to paper! It took me some time to wade through everything just to figure out a system for paying bills. Between working full time in a demanding job and managing two children with multiple extra-curricular lives and growing demands of middle school and high school, I was not eager to take on yet another responsibility that required significant advance planning. I did find a solution: I went to the bank with my parents and they added me to their account so that I could have access to a debit card. It made those little trips to the drugstore for some random item that much easier. When I offered to give my brother and sister monthly reports, they declined. They only wanted to take any burden off me that they could, not wanting to add another task or make it more burdensome.*

*As I've said, for many families, these legal and money issues can tear siblings apart or drive them even further apart. But that was not what occurred for me or for everyone I spoke to. There may have been squabbles, and I'm reflecting on my experience with some rose-colored glasses, to be sure, but I knew my siblings trusted me enough to be the point person. This trust came from childhood, from being raised by parents who were by no means perfect, but who took family life and parenting seriously. All those family times, nightly dinners, chores, traditions, expectations we would get jobs when we could, and witnessing the respect my parents had for each other and for each of us was paying off now. Parenting is definitely a long game.*

Several friends who had been in this situation had given me advice. One told me that one brother who lived out of state was happy to have her take on the management of their parents' needs, while her other brother was not trustworthy. He'd been involved with drugs off and on and was not on good terms with her or their parents at this point. He wasn't a good choice to take on the finances or the healthcare. That made the choice easy for her. She was able to be designated as the Advocate for Healthcare and obtain Power of Attorney over her parents' estate. She told me that having both powers in place made negotiating with doctors and attorneys easier. She also cautioned that I would need to have the documents with me when I went to the emergency room or doctor's office or any other agencies involved in care. She found out the hard way that people want to see paperwork. It was a good heads-up for me. My work-around was having a portable file that I could easily pick up on my way out. If I could go back in time, I might put together an actual "go" bag! I'd include a spare phone charger, earbuds or headphones, a reusable water bottle, comfy socks, some Tylenol and maybe a few granola bars. You never know when you might need to go the emergency room from home or the doctor's office, and those trips are not short.

If you have siblings, consider the situation. How is it? Can you talk without arguing? Is any past damage irreparable or is there room for healing? If you aren't yet at the point where you have to make serious decisions about your parents, can you start mending some fences? It's never too late.

## Your Legacy of Money Mindset

When we think about the legacy a parent might leave behind, we generally think about the money or estate items. But according to financial professionals, there is also the legacy of money mindset. What beliefs and practices around money are being passed down?

Most professionals agree that it's important not only for older people to get their money affairs in order, but for families to discuss money, educate young people on financial responsibility, explain how banks work and how to plan for the future.

When my husband and I got more and more involved caring for my parents, we had a wakeup call. We had two children in late elementary school and middle school, yet we didn't have a Will or any financial plans. We quickly worked with an attorney who specialized in Trusts and Wills, and we put together a family Trust with a Pour-Over Will and outlined our wishes for who would care for our children if something were to happen to us. None of us wants to think about that, but I felt more at ease knowing we had accomplished those tasks.

We also decided to talk with our kids about our wishes. We spent some time telling them how much we loved them, but in loving them, we had to think about what might happen in the event we were not there to care for them. Our children, in fifth grade and eighth grade at the time, were receptive to the conversation. Different timing might be better for your family, and you must make sure you feel that you, your partner, and your kids are able to engage in this sort of conversation. Overall, it's important not to focus on dying, but on how there is a plan and they will not be left without people to care for them.

Now that our children are adults, we've implemented a financial and end-of-life check-up of sorts. We updated our Trust and end-of-life documents, and we talked with our two children about preparing their own Advance Healthcare Directives. They're both legally adults now. In most cases, in an emergency, medical professionals will work with parents of young adults in the event they are unable to communicate their needs. However, it's prudent to have Advance Healthcare Directives due to HIPAA laws. The Health Insurance Portability and Accountability Act (HIPAA) prohibits medical, mental health, and other health service professionals from sharing information with someone other than the patient without written permission. Many estate professionals and lawyers dealing with estates advise parents to direct their young adults to develop legally sound written directives. Each state will have its own laws and forms. Most can be found on a state's legal website, such as the state's attorney general page. It's also fruitful to ask friends or colleagues for recommendations. I found a lot of helpful information on a website called The Balance. This website is a wealth of information about money, banking, and other legal and financial issues. The Balance is part of the "DotDash" publishing group that provides well researched, professional content in a variety of areas. While they do not offer any specific individual advice, they provide a lot of clearly articulated information about some often confusing or complicated topics.

Beyond simply paying attention to legal documents, what else is entailed in the concept of money mindset, and how is this passed on through families?

Money mindset is the overriding belief one has about money, wealth, and finances. Someone with a positive money mindset will view taking action on money issues such as saving, planning, and being a steward of money for a family, as a necessary and fruitful action. Others hold a negative or poverty mindset that there is never enough and that money trouble is inevitable; therefore, actions are not as readily taken. That's a simplified version of money mindset, but it plays into how money is viewed across generations. This can quickly come into play when someone inherits money. It often plays a role in why parents have a difficult time discussing end-of-life planning around money.

It's no wonder there is a slew of money-mindset books, podcasts, and programs to deal with these mindset challenges. Money talks and money concerns tend to be the number one issue in relationships and family dynamics. Our trust attorney and our financial planner both indicated that inheritances and the distribution of assets often brings out the worst in people. There is also that unfortunate tendency for those with money challenges to inherit money and lose it quickly. Financial professionals point to the need for people to adopt wise money-management practices long before a windfall may appear.

Money and legal issues are critical considerations for the sort of legacy we might hope to pass along to our children while we wade through the Sandwich Generation. You're going to have to dig through much of your parents' money and legal issues to be of service to them, but this can also be a trigger to start you thinking about your current situation and how you got there. What beliefs, habits and idiosyncrasies brought you to where you are now? What do you want to consciously or unconsciously pass along to your children? Remember—children are watching and learning by your example!

**“** *Our money biases, our beliefs, and our bugaboos about legal affairs strongly impact our journey inside the Sandwich Generation.* **”**

# 9

# THE IMPORTANCE OF CEREMONY

*Death is only an old door*
*Set in a garden wall*
*On gentle hinges it gives, at dusk*
*When the thrushes call.*

**Nancy Byrd Turner, from "Death is a Door"**

Our lives are filled with all kinds of ceremonies, celebrations, and rituals. They tend to surround and infuse different communities. We have birthday parties, we send holiday cards, we attend graduations, and of course, we attend funerals and memorials. But these take a lot of effort to organize. When you're grieving, it may feel exhausting and time consuming to orchestrate it. Are these ceremonies valuable or necessary?

The research on whether funerals and memorials actually aid in the grief process is thin. Articles written by those in the funeral industry point to the need and well-being benefits, but few scientific studies have explored the effects of funerals on the bereaved member's life afterward. The two most recent studies I found suggest that, in general, people value having a funeral or memorial, but there was not enough research focused directly on whether a funeral impacts, accelerates, or resolves the grief process.

Still, in most cultures, funerals and memorials and grief rituals are expected and encouraged. I never doubted that we would hold a funeral or some type of memorial ceremony for my parents. The tricky part was when.

## Funerals, Memorials, Burials

Every city and most towns have places of worship or funeral homes to facilitate end-of-life ceremonies. The funeral industry is sizable in most western societies. Many, many people and organizations are available to help us pull together a funeral or memorial, and it can be done quickly if need be.

For those who belong to or are connected with a place of worship, there is generally a person or resource available to help arrange funeral or memorial services. If your parent doesn't have a place of worship and you want to hold another type of service, funeral homes offer good guidance. Most funeral homes will honor spiritual practices or even help you to find worship service information. But funeral homes are a business, so make sure you have a sense of what you want before you consult them.

If your parent or you are not particularly religious, there are many ways to hold a memorial service, celebration of life, or commemoration.

What's important is to do something. There may be a feeling that no one will come, or it will only be a few family members, or maybe just you. But holding some sort of memorial or just holding space after the death of a parent is critical to your own healing.

## Grief, Mourning, and Bereavement

Grief is what we experience after loss. It's normal. It's personal. It's a process.

Mourning is what we show on the outside, to the world, to the public. Mourning gives structure to the grief process. It doesn't resolve it, and the grief process, which is personal and internal, will continue. But mourning rituals such as funerals or memorial services allow us to share our grief with others, and to give us comfort. Often, those who are grieving feel they are "going through the motions" during these rituals or ceremonies. However, there is research that consistently points to the positive, long-lasting effects of ritual and ceremony.

Bereavement is the whole process of grief and mourning. We get "bereavement time" from our workplace. People often check in for a period of time to see how we are doing. We get food and flowers and cards. We continue to grieve and work to make sense of the loss.

## Grief Process

Most people feel numb in the immediate aftermath of death. They may be overwhelmed and busy going through the motions and even operating on adrenaline to get everything done. But ritual is important for closure and healing.

Your emotional needs and the emotional needs of your immediate family and your parents' friends and family are served by a time and space to gather and say a final farewell. Death is final. Without a final farewell and acknowledgment, grief can sneak in later and cause a great deal of damage. The ritual of even a very small service or memorial can provide closure that helps us move on. Don't deny yourself or others this necessary step in future healing. Get the support you need from others to put this together if you have not had those conversations already.

## Children and Funerals or Memorials

People often wonder about how much to involve children in these sad times—especially whether they should attend a funeral. The most important person to ask is your child. They can tell you what they can handle, but likely they will want to be with you.

If your child is old enough to attend preschool, then it's appropriate to talk to them about the death of a grandparent or loved one. It's important to acknowledge the death with them. They will notice. They will notice the absence of the person, especially if you have been giving that person a great deal of your time. They will also notice that you are experiencing powerful emotions. While it may seem like talking about death will be traumatic, it's a normal and natural part of life.

Not talking about it can backfire in several ways. Children are always watching us, and they know far more than we think they do. While there are age-appropriate ways to share this information, it's important not to skip it. Holding back can violate trust and compromise security.

A lot of adults worry that death, funerals, and all of this heavy "stuff" is traumatizing for a child. But children also grieve. They grieve in most of the same ways we do. They cry, retreat, and withdraw. Recognize that children have fewer experiences with death and grief, and therefore, quite simply, they don't know what to do. It's not that they don't feel grief; it's more likely that they have fewer coping skills and fewer ways to express their grief and big emotions.

Children may act out big emotions with grief in physical ways. They may cling more, be less able to regulate, be possessive toward a mother or father, or be irritable. They may withdraw into their own world, laugh or try to play in order to avoid the feelings. Children will act in their own way. Acknowledge and accept it. Notice changes in patterns. Changes in behavior are a clue to big emotions.

The next chapter on grief sets out some guidelines about how children deal with grief and the importance of being honest and loving them through the whole process.

Most churches, synagogues, mosques, or other faith organizations have someone who will advise you on the process. They can help you pull together the event and suggest ways to involve children or monitor their needs. Funeral directors or others who help coordinate memorials and celebrations of life also offer this expertise. During this overwhelming time, take advantage of professionals who are there to help.

## Can you involve children in a funeral or ceremony?

In a word: YES. In fact, this might be a good way to help them with their emotions. The key is not to force it. Ask. Children are generally honest and will tell you what they do and do not want to do. It's not a measure of their love if they decline or do not want to participate. Allow for that. However, by no means should you force a child to view a body, kiss a body, or in any way do something that clearly evokes fear.

Yes, it will be upsetting. But being with them, loving them through it rather than denying it, will ultimately be healthier for your child and your family.

## How can you care for your child when you are overcome by grief?

Infants and babies under age two are not likely to comprehend death. But they will likely sense your strong emotions. They can sense that you are not the parent they generally have full access to. This can make them restless. It might be wise to ask a trusted friend, a neighbor, relative, or childcare provider who knows your child to come along to help. This person can hold your child, walk or play with your infant or baby, and give you the space you need to grieve during this difficult time. This can be freeing. Give yourself permission to accept help. While you might feel a need to hold your child, this might not actually be the best for your child at this time. If you believe you will have overwhelming emotions (and this is normal!), that is not necessarily the best energy or emotion for your baby. Infants and babies are sensitive to our moods and emotions. They soak up our energy. Think of those times when you have seen an overwrought mother trying to calm an infant. It's hard to watch! Then a calm partner or friend takes the child and in moments, the child is at ease and may even fall fast asleep. The high and powerful emotions of adults are easily transmitted to others through mirror neurons. Several studies suggest that even very young infants not only imitate an adult caregiver, but exhibit complex cognitive and social skills.

## Older Ages and Stages

Each family must decide for themselves what their children can do and what they can handle in terms of the grief process and funerals. Based on my knowledge of child and human development and years of working with children, here are some basic recommendations about children at funerals or who might be grieving.

Toddlers and children up to about six years of age may need other adults to be on hand to occupy them during a funeral. They may not be able to sit and allow you to participate. It will help them to have some one-on-one adult attention, but more importantly it will help you. This isn't forever—just for the day of the funeral.

In some ways older children can participate more. But still, how do you handle your own grief if they are involved?

School-aged children or older children may be able to participate in some way. You may be able to pair a younger child with an adult or teen and give them a job such as handing out programs, monitoring a guest book, lighting a candle, laying out flowers, or engaging in some other ritual arranged with the church, faith group, funeral home, or other entity helping you with the services.

An older child might sing or play an instrument, read a passage of scripture or poem or remembrance. Find meaningful ways to include an older child, always with their permission. Having a role may actually help older children with their grief process. It keeps them focused and gives importance to their presence. It also helps for them to be busy and not worried about you.

## Nuts and Bolts

Hospice is loving support for many families toward the end of life. I certainly appreciated the care and comfort they provided both my parents and me. There is also a growing profession akin to hospice care, and that is an ***end-of-life doula***.

Most of us think of doulas as someone who helps a woman prepare for the birth of a child, often when a woman chooses to have her child in her home rather than a hospital. They prepare the mother and any partners or family who are on hand. They are there before, during, and after birth to help with process and transitions. They provide immeasurable comfort.

An end-of-life doula is also on hand before, during, and after a death, generally in the home. They may also be called death doulas, end-of-life specialists, or transition guides. Doulas can help prepare the dying person and the family or caregivers on hand. In general, an end-of-life doula is paid for privately, unless employed by a hospice agency. Some end-of-life doulas are also licensed nurses, and Medicare may pay for such nursing services.

I hadn't known about end-of-life doulas. This was new to me, but I think it's a wonderful option. While both my parents lived in an assisted living facility at the time of their deaths, we had the staff and the hospice agency on hand to help us with many aspects of the long process of dying. It strikes me that in the circle of life this process is at the opposite end of birth. It evokes certainty that a momentous and emotional event is to occur, but there is no set timeline—lots of changes to a body, many possible signs, but nothing certain. I relied on the little bits of information staff gave me as I sat holding my father's hand while he died. My mother died in her sleep, so we didn't go through the same process. Just as every birth is unique, so is every death. Someone there to help you know what may happen or to interpret a change that telegraphs a step closer can be comforting.

## Another Day, Another Funeral

One of the things I became aware of while caring for my parents, and what I see happening for other people in my life right now, is that at a certain age, a lot of people die. We know this. It makes sense. It's not just our parents who are aging; their friends are aging, other family members are aging, our friend's parents are aging.

But for those people who are gradually losing their friends, life can feel lonely and surreal. I recall my mom telling me she was the last of her family when her brother died. Later, when I attended the funeral of one of her sorority sisters, she made the comment that there weren't that many of them remaining.

In the early 1950s, my father was a Navy pilot training in Hawaii for the Korean War. My mother had taken a job teaching school at Barber's Point Naval Base just outside of Honolulu. They met and fell in love. My father stayed in touch with the men from his Navy squadron, and eventually my mother got to know each of their wives. An amazing friend group was born. They met now and again until most had retired. Then they started vacationing together every year. In retirement, they traveled together often, discovering new places. The Navy squadron was even invited to my wedding, which was one of their adventures!

Different members of the group began to pass away when most were in their late 70s and early 80s. Each death was felt deeply by the others. I know this was hard for my folks, because I would hear about it and read about it in Christmas cards each year. When my parents began to decline significantly, I wrote to the group to tell them how my parents were doing. I started to hear from each of them when someone died. It was as if the group needed to stay connected and I was now part of the glue.

I raise this issue because eventually I started attending some funerals with my mom. My dad had a harder time moving about once he started using a wheelchair, but my mom wanted to attend funerals. I would drive her to a funeral when I could make the time. It was very important to her to be there for the family and to pay her respects to her friend.

Many older people have told me how difficult it is to be one of the last people standing. Older people go to their friend's funerals often, too. Certainly, they have more time and flexibility, but I think it touches them in a way it might not touch a younger person. It's part of getting prepared. It means as much to the person attending another friend or family member's death as it does to the family.

I thought about this after my parents' memorial. I notified as many people as I could think of, and I was so touched by the folks who came. People came who knew my parents well, and people came who didn't know my parents well, but who knew me. We had the memorial in California, so many of their Ohio friends and family could not be there, but much to my surprise, many of my mother's California relatives came.

Funerals are not for the deceased. Some people come to pay their respects to the person who has died. But many people come for those left behind. Attendance at a funeral is deeply meaningful. A lot of people don't enjoy funerals, but they are healing and valuable for the friends and family who gather.

I go to more funerals now. If I can't go, I am sure to send a card or note and often make a donation in the person's name. That connection is vital for the family who has lost a loved one.

> ❝ *Ritual is important for closure and healing.* ❞

# 10

# GRIEF IS A SNEAKY BEAST

*There is a sacredness in tears. They are not the mark of weakness, but of power. They speak more eloquently than ten thousand tongues. They are messengers of overwhelming grief, of deep contrition, and of unspeakable love.*

**Washington Irving**

Grief doesn't start when your parent dies. In truth, you may experience grief from the moment you recognize that they need you more than you thought. The changes in my parents hit me hard. Selfishly, I missed how much they helped me out. But I also missed how it used to be. I missed their easy laughter, their rich conversation, their activity, and their strength.

I see this often with parents of children who struggle in school. When a child is struggling academically, socially, physically, or emotionally, that's when a school psychologist gets involved. My job is not only to assess the student, but also to work with parents and teachers to develop interventions and accommodations. Sometimes this is Special Education. The bulk of my work as a school psychologist is to conduct psycho-educational assessments to determine eligibility for services. These findings are often painful to share with parents. I don't take it lightly. I work to recognize a child's strengths, not just what is difficult for them. But to tell a parent that their child has significant disabilities, even if they suspect it already, is hard. I have enormous compassion for parents. And while I don't believe a student will never grow or learn, I know that many will struggle. We parents have a vision of our children that is filled with possibility. Most parents assume their child will learn and flourish, just like the other kids. But some will struggle.

When we begin to suspect our parents are not able to manage some tasks that used to be so easy, it's a gut-shot. It hurts. This is when grieving begins.

## My Story

*My mother dies on the day of her 83rd birthday, exactly seven weeks and one day after my father died. It has been a very long seven weeks, and an even longer seven or eight years of caring for them both.*

*My grief journey doesn't hit me immediately. It is tempered by the presence of my brother and nephew who have come in to say goodbye. There were a lot of mixed emotions.*

*My brother and nephew leave early that morning to go visit my mom. At 8:30 a.m., while they are on their way, I get a call from the assisted living facility. They tell me my mother has died in her sleep sometime between 6:00 a.m. and 8:00 a.m. They have only recently confirmed that. At 6:00 a.m. my mother had asked for some water and told a nurse that she was hungry. She ate a banana and drank some water and went back to sleep. At 8:00 a.m. her care manager had stopped in to see her and found her unresponsive. Before calling me, they confirmed her death. Mom was on hospice by that time and she was not resuscitated.*

*I call my brother while he is en route to let him know.*

*My husband and daughter and I quickly dress and head to the facility.*

*Everyone is kind to us. They offer to feed us breakfast, get us coffee. Several staff come by to tell me how much they loved my mom and my dad. We all get a lot of hugs and handshakes.*

*My brother, my husband, and I go into her room see her. She looks like she is asleep. I say goodbye, and I touch her hand. I am unaware what my brother does. I don't know if my nephew comes in to see her. My husband is with me and says his goodbyes. My daughter, nearly 16 now and a sophomore in high school, doesn't want to come in to see her grandmother, even though it is a Saturday and she is not at school. She seems frightened, so I don't push, and I let her know that it is okay.*

*There are things to do. The facility has called hospice and I call the Nautilus Society to send someone to "take the body."*

*My mother is now a body. It feels unkind to say.*

*My mind swims with random thoughts: There are a lot of legal things I must do. They will happen in time. My daughter is with us at the assisted living home. There isn't much for her to do but sit and grieve with us, but she knows we were going to be occupied with so many things, and there is little she can do. I learn there is a lot of waiting around after death. My daughter is especially close to my mother. I worry about her. She is a theater kid and there is a "set build" that she wants to go to after visiting my mom. It suddenly occurs to me that it will be better if she is busy and with friends rather than waiting with us for the coroner's office and the Nautilus Society. There is also the business of packing up my mother's room, something I know she will not want to do.*

*It's strange—I am concerned that I'm not being a good "host" to my brother and nephew. Like I should make sure they are okay.*

*Everything is surreal.*

*My husband takes our daughter to the high school to be with friends and keep her busy. She wants this too.*

*My brother and my nephew find a lobby with the Michigan University football game on, and I make phone calls.*

*When my husband returns, we talk to my brother and the staff about logistics. When do we need to have everything out? We have paid for the month, but if we get everything out early, will there be a refund? Can we donate some things? My dad's wheelchair? Some furniture? Some paintings?*

*I suddenly think about my mother's wedding ring. My husband and my brother and I go in to see if we can take it off her finger.*

*It's a wicked feeling. I feel terrible, and yet, I feel I need to take it, since she will be cremated.*

*We look around the room for any other valuables or items we don't want in the room after she is taken away.*

*I don't remember crying.*

*When the Nautilus Society finally comes to take her, they ask me if I want to see her one last time. I decline. I have said my goodbyes. It was easier for me to have said goodbye when she was in her bed rather than saying goodbye now, when they are getting ready to take her.*

*The staff of the Nautilus Society is outstanding, patient and kind and sensitive. They are aware that my mother was regarded with much love, and they treat all of us with kindness and warmth.*

*The staff of the assisted living is wonderful, as well. They keep checking on us. All the staff come to talk to me. They are most accommodating about when we can gather her belongings, too. I know, though, that they have a long waiting list and will need the room.*

*The next day, my brother and nephew will come to help us move furniture and heavy items. They will fly back home Sunday afternoon, so we must work to get as much out Sunday morning as possible.*

*Following the removal of my mother's body, and after I call one more time to check on my daughter, we all go to an Irish pub for our own little family wake. We talk about the funny things my dad used to say or the crazy life events over the years. We share many stories—almost exclusively fun ones or ones that make us laugh.*

*For me, grief has been a sneaky beast that creeps in at inopportune times. It could be at a time of great joy, but the little beast reminds me that I am missing someone I love who used to share in this joyous event—Christmas Eve dinner; a favorite movie we shared on Netflix; a phrase that makes me hear my dad's voice or my mom's laugh. That's all it takes, and tears fill my eyes. Grief also visits me in times of stress when I think, "I should ask Mom what she would do," or, "Now what was the secret to that recipe?" or, "What did Dad always tell me that noise in the car means?"*

Grief is a process. It doesn't hit everyone the same way, and there are several theories about stages or types of grief. Perhaps the most well-known is the stage theory of grief by Elisabeth Kubler-Ross, who authored the seminal text, *On Death and Dying.* There are more recent studies, but most grief researchers still pull from her theory to some extent.

- **Denial.** Shock and denial can thrust us into a state of overwhelm and make us feel like life is meaningless, but it also paces our grief. It gives us time to ask the hard question: Why? Denial prepares us to move through our grief.

- **Anger**. Anger is a vital and necessary emotion in our healing process. It's important to feel it and acknowledge it, even if it seems unreasonable. Anger often masks pain, but it's an emotion with a lot of energy that can move us through our grief. Anger is a bridge through grief and a reflection of the intensity of our love.

- **Bargaining.** After a death, we may bargain that if we change our life or dedicate ourselves to some worthy cause, then we can wake up and realize this has been a dream. We ask a lot of "what if" questions in this phase, and guilt can accompany our bargaining. We may even bargain with the pain, hoping that will take it away.

We move in and out of stages, back and forth, minutes, sometimes days. It's not linear.

- **Depression.** Depression is normal and natural and not a sign of mental illness. Losing a loved one is depressing. Not to experience some level of depression would be unusual, so know that it is a normal stage that may take some time to move past.

- **Acceptance.** It's important to realize acceptance does not mean we suddenly feel okay about our loss. We may never feel okay, but we can reach a place where we accept the finality of death and realize our loved one is not coming back. We learn to live with the loss, remembering our loved one; but we learn to accept and embrace the new normal that emerges in our loved one's absence.

Kubler-Ross studied people who were in the process of dying, and her research occurred decades ago. These five stages she identified are what people who were terminally ill might experience. But psychologists have found that these stages also describe the grief process of someone losing a loved one. Kubler-Ross's frequent co-author and mentee, David Kessler, has continued her work and is considered one of the foremost experts on death and grief. In 2019 he wrote *Finding Meaning: The Sixth Stage of Grief*, which more deeply explores the stages but also presents a sixth stage he calls "finding meaning." Kessler details his own grief journey following the death of his adult son. He is also the founder of Grief.com, a rich website that explains more about research on death, dying, and grief. He dispels the myth that the stages are lockstep. Some people may not experience all of these stages or emotions, but they will generally go through some process when grieving. It is most important to realize that whatever you feel, whether it seems rational or not, is valid. Recognizing that grief impacts each of us uniquely is important.

I personally don't recall a bargaining stage. My parents were older and had medical concerns, and I know rationally that we all die. If I bargained at all, it might have been for more time.

I did experience anger. It was hard for me to hear people talk about their grandmother who was 95 or 101 and "still going strong, mind clear as a bell." Why did that person get more time with their loved one? Why couldn't my mother and father live into their hundreds and have minds as clear as a bell? I was angry and jealous.

The feeling of depression was horrible. When my brother and nephew left a few days after my mom died, we went back to everyday life. We had decided to have a joint memorial service later in the year, when my siblings and their families could all be together. We had to coordinate school schedules, airline schedules, and all the details. But going back to everyday life was hard. How could we just go on as if nothing were different? Just going to the grocery store was hard for me. My grief felt like a heavy fur coat in the middle of the hot, dry September in Sacramento. *It's 101° in the shade and Christy's draped in a fur coat. What's wrong with her?* That's how depression felt for me.

I also believed that everyone should or would know I had just lost my parents, as if there were a tattoo across my forehead: "Caution! Just lost both parents!" When I'd see a friend or acquaintance who I thought surely knew, but who offered no words of comfort, I felt irritated, offended, hurt, overlooked. I know it's difficult to say something to someone we know is grieving. We hold back because we don't want to open a wound. I have since heard from many, many people that some acknowledgment is better than none. I would agree. The wound is there. Acknowledgment doesn't open it further; it seems to have the opposite effect. Acknowledgment or a hug is an offer of comfort, an effort to staunch the wound. It helps. And if there are tears, know that your words or gesture didn't cause them. The tears are ever ready. It's a gift to feel you can let the tears go with someone kind enough and brave enough to witness your grief.

I don't think it's best to offer your own meaning or try to tell someone that time will heal, or it's for the best, or she's in a better place. While generally well-meaning, these phrases are not helpful, because they come from a place of fear, unease, or anxiety from the giver. You really don't know how the grieving person feels unless you ask, and do you really need to ask, or is it best to simply let them know you care? I, myself, have said those things before. Now I try to hold off and simply let them know I care. If appropriate, I offer to be available to help. The point is, letting someone know you acknowledge their grief in simple terms is a caring act.

Grief sneaks up on us in the details, as well, and there were lots of little details to attend to—death certificates, memorial plans, estate disbursements, and closing accounts. I bounced from denial to anger to and depression for quite some time. Even now, after nearly five years, that nasty little grief beast sneaks up on me. I don't wear it like a fur coat any longer. I dodge it like a wave at the shore. I don't let it pull me under, but I feel its power and force.

## Talking with Children About Grief

Talking about death is difficult for many. With children, it can be a big concern. Do we tell the kids? If so, how?

Grief is also difficult. It's hard to be in your own grief journey and also consider how to comfort your children or spouse in their grief.

Probably the most important thing, for you as well as the rest of the family, is to open lines of communication. All feelings are normal, and it's important to communicate about the loss of a grandparent or parent or any loved one.

Be aware of developmental stages. You know your child or children. After age 4 or 5, use the words, died or death and avoid phrases such as, "passed away" or "gone to sleep." These are unclear and can cause confusion. Imagine a child thinking a grandparent will return at any time, or fears for you when you go to sleep? Death is natural. They may not fully understand the concept initially, but as they age and encounter other deaths—a pet, another relative, a friend's relative—then they will come to a healthy understanding of death.

Here are some guidelines based on child development research:

- Preschool-aged children (up to five years of age) may view death as temporary, like a cartoon character that gets knocked down but gets back up again. They don't easily understand the finality of death. They may seem uninterested or like they don't fully grasp the significance. This is normal, and it's okay. Speak in clear, concrete terms, but don't belabor the point. There is no need to drive home the finality of it if they seem resistant.

- School-aged children from about five to nine can grasp the finality of death, but it's still somewhat abstract. They understand that living things die, but it may seem remote from them and somewhat impersonal. They may conceptualize death as a skeleton. They may have nightmares. Support them by encouraging them to talk about their feelings.

- From about age nine on through adolescence, children have a concept of death as a final and concrete state. They can be acutely conscious of how others around them feel. It may help them to talk to someone other than the grieving adults in order to process their feelings. This is also normal and okay. Our children often want to care for us, but they may not be able to give us what we need. In this regard, having another adult to support them will help you get your needs met.

People, no matter their age or stage, are unique, and each person experiences grief in a different way.

This is part of the sunset, too, moving from the warm and colorful glow to the darkness. The darkness spreads and most of us sleep. We need that down time before the sun rises again the next day. Grief is also necessary. It is part of the transition from life as we know it one way, to life as it will be from here on. Taking time to honor it, even though painful, is healing.

Keep in mind your own grief. You may not be able to give the level of comfort that your child needs. They still need you, and they need to know you will be okay, but this is a good time to call on others for help. Get help for yourself and have friends or other family members alert school counselors, if necessary.

I wish I had been better at asking for help. I wish I had called my daughter's school and alerted them so that a teacher or counselor could have touched base with her. I asked her if she wanted me to, but of course, at 15 she said no. I wish I'd been more persistent.

Like most people, kids don't always know what is best for them, but as parents, sometimes we have an obligation to override their judgment for their well-being. But my judgment was clouded with my own grief. My husband was focused on me and he had his own grief, so we both sort of checked in with her, but I know we didn't give her all that she needed just then.

She told me several years later that it had been tough for her. She knew I was hurting, so she didn't want to come to me. My son, her brother, was two thousand miles away at college, and she didn't want to call him. Her father, my husband, was focused on me, grieving himself, and busy with daily to-do lists. My daughter felt alone. She didn't want to tell people at school. She told me later she that she sometimes felt nauseous after eating and would make herself throw up. I recall at the time asking her if she was okay, but she always said she was fine. I heard what I wanted to hear. We've talked much about it over the last few years, and she says she thinks that was her grief response. She didn't want to burden me, but she was hurting inside. It lasted a couple of months but has not become a pattern.

I spoke with her about including this in the book, and she said she learned about her own need to cope differently. I asked her if she would have been upset if I had called her school and let them know about her grandmother's death. She said she would still have told me "no" if I asked, but she would not have been upset if I'd done it anyway.

Here you have it straight from the mouth of teenager—a powerful endorsement for sharing information!

My daughter has since rebounded beautifully. She is even more resilient in the face of challenge. We talk openly and often about my mother, and she has begun researching our family ancestry. She always loved my mother's stories about her childhood during World War II and the Great Depression. Recently my daughter started collecting stories from my husband's parents in an effort to gather and savor as much as she can about her whole family. She recognizes that death is part of life, even though painful and sad.

My biggest take-away and advice is to honor your grief process. Grief can last for a long time; there is no "normal" length of grieving time. We generally return to routine, to friends and family and work. However, some people don't move on from grief and can develop symptoms of what is known as "complicated grief." If normal signs of grief seem to get worse or heighten, especially after a year, I recommend you seek help. Symptoms might include:

- Focus on little else but your deceased love one, or intense rumination on the loss of your loved one

- Extreme focus on reminders of your loved one, or avoidance of reminders of your loved one

- Problems accepting the death

- Loss of interest in living; suicidal thoughts

- Can't get out of bed

- Can't sleep for prolonged amounts of time

- Can't eat

- Overeating more than normal

- Lack of basic hygiene

- Not interested in seeing people for prolonged amounts of time or even briefly

- Unable to focus or care for your children

- Unable to go back to work

These are signs that you might need to seek help. Grief can be a long process, but you should be able to return to increased levels of functioning in your life. There is help, and there are several ways to connect with support groups.

Faith-based organizations often have grief support groups, and most physicians can direct you to local community-based organizations that have grief support groups if the health plan does not. See the Resource section of this book for additional options.

**"*Grief sneaks up to us in the details.*"**

# 11

# NEXT CHAPTER: JOURNEY TO SUNRISE

*What do you get from loss? You get awareness of other people's loss, which allows you to connect with that other person, which allows you to love more deeply and to understand what it's like to be a human being if it's true that all humans suffer.*

Stephen Colbert

*What I know for sure is that every sunrise is like a new page, a chance to right ourselves and receive each day in all its glory. Each day is a wonder.*

Oprah Winfrey

## My Story

*Because I lived minutes from my parents, I got the stuff. All of the stuff. At one point I felt like I had inherited my entire childhood home.*

*When my parents first moved into assisted living, a lot of their furniture, family pictures, cherished artwork, and personal items went with them. We held an estate sale, and what wasn't sold was donated, but there were a lot of things my mother, especially, could not part with. Two items stand out in my memory.*

*One was a pair of brass conquistador stirrups.*

*The other was an 8 x 10 framed portrait of Jesus.*

*The conquistador stirrups are heavy, brass, and curly toed stirrups into which, presumably, a conquistador would shove his booted foot while atop a proud stallion on the way to conquer, plunder, and ransack some new land. Just the sort of item everyone wants in their home (yes, I'm being sarcastic!). For some reason, my mother loved them. I believe they were her mother's. I recall her getting them after my grandfather died. She hung them up on the wall and inserted flowing, plastic ivy. She was so proud to have them, as if she had been waiting to inherit them. Art to behold, for sure.*

*The framed portrait of Jesus hung in my parents' bedroom for as long as I can remember. In my mind's eye, I still see the dried palm frond from a Palm Sunday stuck between the wall and the hanging picture of a longhaired, beautiful man. He traveled with them from Ohio to California and from their home to two different assisted living facilities.*

*Along with Jesus and the stirrups, I inherited the costume jewelry in my mother's battered jewelry box, my father's assorted tie tacks and personalized golf ball markers, boxes of family photos, framed family pictures, a camel-backed loveseat my mother had inherited from her father and which she made me promise would stay in the family, and what seemed like a million pounds of paperwork.*

*I found files that held yellowing pages of old cartoons cut from newspapers and magazines over the years, Time magazines, and newspapers reporting moon landings and other historical events, all my mom's and dad's college yearbooks, two silver-plated tea service sets, and several blue, four-fold, commemorative-state quarter sets.*

*After my parents' deaths, my sister, brother, and I went through a lot of things together, but since they both lived out of state, they didn't take much with them. I sent them what they wanted, but I ended up with the lion's share, not really because I wanted all of it, but because I was there. Proximity has its drawbacks.*

*The final distribution of most of the valuable items such as jewelry, artwork, or other meaningful items was doled out per my parents' wishes. A lot of my mother's jewelry had been dispersed before or just after she went into assisted living. My mother and sister and I had talked, joked, and bargained over some items for years. I wanted the heirloom diamond and sapphire ring, since it had "always" gone to the oldest daughter, which was meaningless for my mom, who was the only daughter, but that meant my sister got the diamond necklace and earrings because she had two daughters. My sister wanted a beautiful set of cable car prints and I wanted some of my grandmother's prizewinning needlepoints. My brother wanted some of my dad's navy flight wings as well as his precious set of MacGregor Persimmon woods and a few other golf clubs. We had talked openly with our parents about these treasures. One Christmas, my sister and I teased my mom and dad by racing through the house and marking what we wanted with Post-It notes, including a classic Nabisco Saltine tin. My sister got to that one first!*

*Since we had talked about a lot of these items for years, there was no need to quarrel at the end. I took apart several of my mother's broken necklaces and charm bracelets and restrung them with other beads and charms and made bracelets for all the women in the immediate family: my sister, my sister in-law, the three granddaughters, a grandniece, and a soon-to-be-grandniece. For the men of the family, I set out memorabilia and encouraged them to comb through the golf tees and tie tacks and other assorted items and take what they wanted.*

*But when everyone was gone after my parents' final memorial, I was left with everything else. We sold coins and I sent checks to my siblings, and then I started the painful process of breaking down the boxes of stuff and beginning to throw items away.*

*Pictures were the hardest. I scanned what I thought was important to keep, I sent some to my brother and sister, but I tossed quite a few. I kept important documents such as tax returns, a binder of current bills, and anything that might be useful if some sort of legal issue arose. But I threw away a lot of pictures.*

*I couldn't bear to throw away the college yearbooks, the conquistador stirrups, and the framed photo of Jesus.*

This is a task that falls to children and families after someone dies. It's folded in with the grief process and compounded with interest when both parents pass away, and a family home full of memories and mementos and history is disbursed. Sometimes the home itself is passed along to someone, but many times, the home and all that it holds must be sold. Not only is that a monumental task in terms of time, organization, coordination, effort, and expense, but it can be heart wrenching. If you don't need to sell the house immediately, I advise taking some time to simply prepare yourself. Give yourself time to go through things at your own pace. Have others help you sort. Sometimes it's nice to acknowledge or tell the story of an item before you let it go.

I've heard of many creative ideas since I went through my parents' belongings. I liked the idea of taking a video of yourself with an item or set of items and telling the story of them, then sharing the video with family. You might discover a family member who wants to take something off your hands. There is a lot of family history to be shared.

## Keeping Family Together

My brother-in-law Paul, after his mother died several years after his father, recommended we proactively find times to reunite and get together. For many years he was able to meet with siblings who were spread across the country, because the unifying connection of parents and caring for an aging parent brought them together. Now, he said, that same "need" no longer existed. He took it upon himself to coordinate family gatherings, because it helped keep them all in touch on a deeper level.

This is a phenomenon of the latter part of the 20th century and into the 21st century here in the United States. Americans are highly mobile. People move an average of 11 times over the course of their lives. More people are moving away from their hometown after high school or college or time in the military. We're spread out. Sure, we have smartphones and social media, but family culture and family history are best cultivated in person.

Find ways to reunite. In addition to weddings and graduations and funerals, create fun times with less stress. Do a quick drive-through to say hello or to spend a weekend together. Staying in touch is good not only for your soul but also for the children. Most children love to hear stories about their parents' and grandparent's childhoods. As they get older, they also love to hear the stories of their own childhood. Be sure to tell these stories—within reason. No need to pass on stories that humiliate or shame. Listen to your children and pay attention to their reactions.

## Building a Legacy of Love

This time in the Sandwich Generation is rich. The lessons we learn don't reveal themselves right way. Our memories gently age and shift, and we learn to let go of the painful times and move beyond grief.

After some time, we can look back and try to make sense of it all.

A year or so after my parents' passing, I was able to forgive myself for times I wasn't my best as a daughter, sibling, parent, or spouse. I could acknowledge that I'd done my best and not beat myself up. I became a better parent, too, connecting again with my children as young adults who had been through the journey with me. We still talk a lot of Grandma and Grandpa, and my children have been willing and supportive consultants on this book.

With time, I could also see how I had changed for the better. I learned a lot of lessons from my parents. One of the best gifts they gave me was planning for the end of their lives. They made the tough choices, so their children didn't have to: assisted living, cremation services, burial at a National Cemetery, Catholic mass. They also put enough money aside for their care. My siblings and I didn't have to accrue debt, and that was for us the gift of freedom. We were and are lucky. This isn't the case for everyone.

My husband and I have spent time trying to do the same for our children. We talk about our wishes for the future and for end of life. We try to normalize conversations about end-of-life issues so that our kids can ask questions or at least feel comfortable knowing we are not leaving everything up to them.

But we don't know exactly what tough choices they will still have to make. Which one of them will have that painful car-key conversation with us?

We also emphasize our value of compassion. How does compassion continue to show up in their lives? How are we continuing to be compassionate with others in our lives?

What I learned while writing this book, through the tears and the frustrations, is that people naturally want to give and want to have a way to contribute to others. I probably already knew this, but it was driven home as I wrote this book. I look back on how much my parents gave me, but also how much my children have given me and the contributions made by others.

You will take many gifts from this journey. May it be a Legacy of Love.

# Summary

There is so much more to say. I continue to learn more and more about the Sandwich Generation, parenting, what it takes to be a steward of a legacy of love. But as I've said, I wrote the book I wish I'd had, and here is where this piece ends.

- Seek clarity for yourself first. Envision sitting somewhere and enjoying a perfect sunset with your parents and family. What do you need to do to generate that feeling?

- Take time to meditate or pray before critical conversations—then rehearse.

- Think like a case manager—assemble a crack team of experts to help you along the way.

- Be gentle with yourself. While you are definitely a superhero, you aren't perfect, and striving to be so is unhealthy.

- Remember to take time to practice or embrace spirituality, as you know it.

- Seek professional help about money, legal, and mental health issues—and get it all in writing.

- Your children will also grow from this time and will grow in strength along with you.

- Seek personal help, support and guidance. You do NOT have to do everything yourself.

- Consider what legacy you want to pass along to your children. Then focus on that. Your instincts will lead the way when you take time to quiet yourself to hear them.

**"*Find ways to reunite.*"**

# AFTERWORD

You've loved your parent. You've nudged, managed, cared, consoled, comforted, cried, and said goodbye.

So many aspects of sunset: Afterglow, blue hour, dusk, twilight.

What do you envision when you look toward the inevitable sunset for your parents or even for yourself? What colors do you imagine as the most brilliant, the most radiant, and the ones that take your breath away? If you could paint it, how would it look? Who is with you? How do you want to feel? What memories can become the movies of your dreams?

Pondering the sunset and your experience of it, getting a feel for the moments that lie ahead, does not have to be morbid. In fact, taking time to consciously ponder can inspire you to plan now. It can lead you to create the most exquisite sunset.

Orange. Red. Purple. Blue.

The choice is yours. Be colorful. Be creative. Be compassionate.

Be love.

# APPENDIX

In addition to attending to the "stuff" and the legal issues, here are some specific tasks that will arise and demand attention quickly. It may be wise to identify someone to assist you with these tasks—someone who can help you stay on track when it gets tough.

## Must Dos

Handle these critical tasks quickly.

- Get at minimum ten death certificates. Various agencies will need them, and some will require originals. Always ask if a copy is acceptable, but keep at least ten on hand, just in case. Obtaining an original can take a few days, so avoid delay by having a stockpile.

- Notify the Department of Motor Vehicles. Even if your parent was no longer driving at the time of their death, they likely had an identification card. Notify the DMV as soon as possible to avoid identity theft.

- Notify the Social Security office.

- Notify banks and other financial institutions, including mortgage lenders.

- Cancel credit cards AND notify all credit reporting agencies—Equifax, Experian, and TransUnion. Send a certified letter to each of these agencies with a request to flag the account with the statement, "Deceased: Do not offer or extend credit." Also get a copy of a credit report to know exactly what debts are current.

- Cancel online social media accounts and websites owned by your parent.

- Notify the post office and request a forward to your address so you can cancel incoming magazines and other periodic mailings.

- Notify the local election board.

- Cancel membership in organizations such as sororities, fraternities, professional organizations, etc.

- Notify your parents' accountant or tax preparer, if they have one.

- Notify your parents' financial planner or advisor, if they have one.

## Record Keeping

Life generates a lot of paper, and much of it we are tempted to toss in the garbage. Before you do that, know what records are important to keep for a period of time.

Most sources suggest keeping tax returns for at least seven years. Some sources suggest keeping medical records for five years. If you keep it all together, seven years will likely serve you well. Of course, feel free to purge medical records after five years if they are taking up a lot of room.

After five years, I still get mail for my parents, such as magazine subscriptions, and I take time to contact the company and let them know my folks no longer need the publication.

After a year had passed since their deaths, I still got bills. There is a statute of limitations on debt collections, but these vary by state. Consult the Consumer Protections Bureau before sending off a check or taking legal action. See the Resources section for contact information.

Medical bills continued to trickle in for a year after my parents' deaths. For that reason, I did not close their bank account (for which I was a signer) for several years. However, there is a limit to how long medical providers can collect on a debt. For more information, go to the Debt.Org site listed in the Resources section.

# ACKNOWLEDGMENTS AND GRATITUDE

I am blessed and incredibly grateful that there are so many people on my thank-you list.

First, I thank Peggy and Charlie Byrne, my parents, who were great role models for parenting and for life. Now, over five years after their passing, I still miss them every day, and writing this book made me truly grateful for their wisdom, the gifts they gave me and my siblings by being good stewards of money, making tough decisions before they needed to so we wouldn't have to, and for always loving us unconditionally.

I thank my siblings, Kelley and Steve, who were always supportive. Thank you for trusting me. Thank you for showing up whenever I called and for making time for visits and calls and emails and texts. I love you both.

I thank my husband, Brad. I do not have enough words to express my depth of appreciation for all your love, support, and encouragement every step of the way—not just in the writing of this book, but also in dearly caring for my parents.

I thank my children, MacGregor and Bailey. You two are my greatest joys in life. You humble me with your amazing talents, immeasurable compassion, delicious humor, and love.

I thank my Yates Family—The Yates Crew— for all your kindness, support, friendship, humor, and always accepting me as I am. I'm so blessed that my "in-law" family is all of you. Jane and Don, you've built a Legacy of Love for all of us.

For the Bees, Amy, Christina, and Suze! Thanks for all the love, advice, not allowing me to quit, incredible editing and technical support, and for being a ton of fun, to boot. Let's keep writing.

Thank you to Jan Fishler and Jodi Brandon for great developmental edits and support. I couldn't have done it without your talents. Thank you to Nina Durfee, editor and Andy Meaden, book designer, who made my words sound and look fabulous. No small feat! I appreciate your willingness to hold the hand of a first-time author.

I thank all of my friends whom I've spent hours talking to and who have been on this journey or are embarking on it now—wow! Thank you for your stories, your input, your generous advice, your tears. Thank you for sharing all of the joys, frustrations, and pains. I hope that you all continue to build Legacies of Love with your families.

Thank you to caregivers everywhere who work with elderly people. Thank you for all you do. When I started writing this book, I already had enormous admiration for your skills and talents. But now, having lived through 2020 and the COVID-19 Pandemic, I know you to be angels on earth. I am forever grateful.

# RESOURCES

A number of resources helped me as I cared for my parents, and I've discovered even more while writing this book. I'm sure there are more I don't know about yet. But here is what I have to share:

## Helpful Websites

### Broad Based Information on Aging

- AARP: All things about retirement and aging. A classic.

  **https://www.aarp.org**

- **A Place for Mom**: This organization is excellent and provides a great deal of actionable information, not only about places to live but where to find a wealth of information. The website has up-to-date information for a number of large cities in the U.S. While their website is informative, they do tend to flood you with emails or calls if you use them for your only source for finding residential placement.

  **https://www.aplaceformom.com**

- **National Council on Aging**: This organization is a big clearinghouse and can give you some broad-based information. Many states have their own councils on aging, and you might want to put your state's name and "council on aging" in a search engine to find more local resources.

  **https://www.ncoa.org**

- **Next Avenue:** This website offers a range of information, research, support, and useful information for seniors and for caregivers.

  **https://www.nextavenue.org**

- **SeniorLiving.org**: Another broad-based information site that offers good resources.

  **https://www.seniorliving.org**

- **U.S. Department of Health and Human Services**: A good resource, but very broad-based. A good go-to for some legal guidelines.

  **https://www.hhs.gov/aging/index.html**

- **California Department of Aging:** I live in California, so I include that link here, but most, if not all states do have resources for aging.

  **https://www.aging.ca.gov**

## *Professionals in Caregiving and Case Management*

- **Aging Care**: This website has a locator tool to find geriatric case managers.

  **https://www.agingcare.com/local/geriatric-care-managers**

- **Certified Senior Advisors**: Broad based with a feature under the resources tab where you can locate a certified senior advisor near you. A Certified Senior Advisor offers give support in a variety of areas.

  **https://www.csa.us/**

## *Funerals, Burials, and Alternatives to Funerals and Burials*

- **Funeral Consumer Alliance**: Offers details for finding a funeral home, planning, financing, and legal issues.

  **https://funerals.org/?consumers=choose-funeral-home**

- Tips on Funeral Planning from AARP

  **https://www.aarp.org/home-family/friends-family/info-2020/funeral-planning-tips.html**

- Funeral Planning Checklist from AgingCare.com

  **https://www.agingcare.com/articles/funeral-planning-checklist-145646.htm**

- **Better Place Forest**: An alternative to cemetery burial, a Better Place Forest is currently operating in California and Arizona and will join cremated remains with the earth surrounding a specific, chosen tree.

  **https://www.betterplaceforests.com**

- **Cake:** This unique company and website could go in several sections. It offers information about end-of-life wishes documentation, advance health care directives, and a large repository of links to a whole host of end-of-life concerns. Here's the home page link and the blog link, which offers interesting alternatives to burial:

  **https://www.joincake.com**

  **https://www.joincake.com/blog/burial-alternatives-for-nontraditional-people**

## *Grief*

- Grief.com

  **https://grief.com**

- Center for Grief Recovery and Therapeutic Resources

  **https://griefcounselor.org/resources/helpful-websites**

- The Dougy Center: The National Center for Grieving Children and Families

  **https://www.dougy.org/grief-resources**

## Financial Support

- **Consumer Protections Bureau**: CPB can help with financial issues such as bills and fraud.

  **https://www.credit.com/debt/statutes-of-limitations**

- **Debt.org**: Another good site for financial help. It provides information on how long debts can be collected.

  **https://www.debt.org/advice/deceased-relatives**

- **Financial Planning Association:** How to find a Certified Financial Planner—self-explanatory. If you need more support in developing a Trust or Will, and you don't have any referrals in your area, start here.

  **http://www.plannersearch.org**

## Self-Care and Support

**ChristyYates.com:** My website offers a number of resources for folks in the Sandwich Generation. You can find the Self-Assessment from Chapter 3 there as well as other strategies mentioned in this book.

**https://christyyates.mykajabi.com**

For over 900 Free Tapping Videos, my husband, Brad Yates's site is the number one place to visit.

**https://www.youtube.com/tapwithbrad**

**Melody Beattie:** Her website could go in a couple of sections here, but she offers some of the best information and support for self-development, co-dependency, support, and grief.

**https://melodybeattie.com**

- Special thanks to two individuals who helped me so much with legal and financial information:

Stephan M. Brown, Esquire
NewPoint Law Group, LLP
**www.newpointlaw.com**

Carol Hunter
The Money Mender
**www.themoneymender.com**

## Self-Assessment

- Challenges of the Sandwich Generation

Take a deep breath and consider each statement and rate yourself on a scale of 1 to 5, with 1 being "Strongly Disagree" and 5 being "Strongly Agree." (see over)

| | | 1. Strongly Disagree | 2. Disagree | 3. Neither Agree nor Disagree | 4. Agree | 5. Strongly Agree |
|---|---|---|---|---|---|---|
| 1. | I am emotionally ready and willing to take on this challenge. | | | | | |
| 2. | I understand my parents' current physical health needs. | | | | | |
| 3. | I understand my parents' current emotional needs. | | | | | |
| 4. | I am aware of my parents' current financial needs and am equipped to manage them. | | | | | |
| 5. | I am ready and able to balance raising my children while caring for my parents. | | | | | |
| 6. | I recognize that I am the one person who can do most of this work. | | | | | |
| 7. | I feel calm, loving acceptance of the tasks ahead. | | | | | |
| 8. | I have strong habits in place to take care of my emotional and physical needs. | | | | | |
| 9. | Right now in my life, I have the support I need to take on this challenge. | | | | | |
| 10. | Other family members are ready and willing to help me in this challenge. | | | | | |

Review your ratings and revisit these questions often. Your answers will change. Do common themes arise? Do you have more questions about WHAT to do than about your WILLINGNESS to take on the challenge? Do you have the support you need? Are other family members supportive of your efforts?

Knowledge Base:   Total from questions 1 – 4   _____

Stress Status:   Total from questions 5 –10   _____

## Where do you fit? Where do you want to go?

## LEGACY OF RESENTMENT

Family learns:

- elder care is a burden
- resentment toward others frustration
- systems inconsistent

*Continuum of Stress*

## LEGACY OF LOVE

Family learns:

- Love = compassion and caring
- acceptance that people contribute what they can
- consistent, congruent systems in place

*Continuum of Knowledge*

## LEGACY OF CHAOS

Family learns:

- elder care is overwhelming
- it's harmful to others
- most members suffer
- few systems in place

## LEGACY OF OBLIGATION

Family learns:

- Elder care is complicated
- better left to others
- sense of powerlessness
- systems incongruent

# BIBLIOGRAPHY

**Just a note:** Some of these books I read specifically to learn more for this book. The book by Atul Gwande, M.D., for example, helped me during my time in the Sandwich Generation and as I wrote this book. Several books have informed my professional and personal life over the years and were the foundation for my thoughts on mindset, the legacy matrix, and how to move from a "stuck" place to one of freedom.

Bridges, William. 1991. *Managing Transitions: Making the Most of Change.* Reading, Mass: Addison-Wesley.

Dweck, Carol S. 2006. *Mindset: The New Psychology of Success.* New York: Random House.

Gawande, Atul. *Being Mortal: Medicine and What Matters in the End.* First edition. New York: Metropolitan Books: Henry Holt & Company, 2014.

Kessler, David. 2019. *Finding Meaning: The Sixth Stage of Grief.* New York: Simon & Schuster.

Patterson, Kerry. 2012. *Crucial Conversations: Tools for Talking When Stakes Are High.* New York: McGraw-Hill.

Wickert, Kimberly McCrone, Danielle Schultz Dresden, and Phillip D. Rumrill. 2013. *The Sandwich Generation's Guide to Eldercare.*

# ABOUT THE AUTHOR

Christy Yates is a passionate advocate for children and parents. She is a licensed educational psychologist, writer, speaker, and coach. She coaches Sandwich Generation parents to manage the chaos and overwhelm of raising kids while caring for aging parents, so they can show up powerfully and joyfully for themselves and their families. She also produces content and workshops on the topics of self-care, special education, and parenting issues. During 2020 and 2021 she's spoken to several schools and parent groups about motivation and resilience in the time of COVID19. She lives in Northern California with her husband and cat and enjoys occasional, yet glorious, visits from their grown children.

*To learn more or to engage the services of Christy Yates Byrnes, visit:*

# www.ChristyYates.com

# ENDNOTES

## Preface

[1] Angela Stringfellow, "Caregiver 101: What is the Sandwich Generation?" Seniorlink Blog, January 17, 2018, https://www.seniorlink.com/blog/sandwichgenerations#:~:text=In%201982%2C%20social%20worker%20Dorothy,of%20their%20own%20aging%20parents.

[2] Kim Parker and Eileen Patton. "Sandwich Generation: Rising Financial Burdens for Middle-Aged Americans," Pew Research Center https://www.pewsocialtrends.org/2013/01/30/the-sandwich-generation/#a-profile-of-the-sandwich-generation.

[3] T. Rowe Price 2019. PRESS RELEASE: T. Rowe Price: Sandwich Generation Strain Negatively Impacts Kids and Their Money Habits. Accessed December 29, 2020. https://www.troweprice.com/corporate/us/en/press/t--rowe-price--sandwich-generation-strain-negatively-impacts-kid.html.

[4] Center For Disease Control (CDC) National Vital Statistics Reports (NVSS). Accessed March 23, 2020. https://www.cdc.gov/nchs/products/nvsr.htm

[5] Centers for Disease Control and Prevention. Life Expectancy. Accessed March 23, 2020. https://www.cdc.gov/nchs/fastats/life-expectancy.htm.

[6] Cubanski, Juliette, Wyatt Koma, Anthony Damico, and Tricia Newuman. 2018. "How many seniors live in poverty?" *Kaiser Family Foundation*, November 19, 2018. https://www.kff.org/medicare/issue-brief/how-many-seniors-live-in-poverty/.

[7] Artiga, Samantha, Jennifer Tolbert, Jennifer Kates, Josh Michaud, and Kendal Orgera. 2020. "Growing COVID-19 hotspots in the U.S. south and west will likely widen disparities for people of color. Kaiser Family Foundation, July 10, 2020. https://www.kff.org/policy-watch/growing-covid-19-hotspots-in-south-and-west-likely-widen-disparities-people-of-color/.

[8] American Psychological Association. 2015. "Stress in America: Paying with Our Health." Accessed December 15, 2020. https://www.apa.org/news/press/releases/stress/2014/stress-report.pdf.

[9] Reinhard, Susan, Lynn Friss Feinberg, Ari Houser, Rita Choula, and Molly Evans. 2019. "Valuing the Invaluable: Charting a Path Forward." *AARP Public Policy Institute*. November 14, 2019. https://www.aarp.org/ppi/info-2015/valuing-the-invaluable-2015-update.html.

[10] Brody, Debra J., Quiping Gu. 2020. "Antidepressant Use Among Adults: United States, 2015-2018." *Centers for Disease Control and Prevention*. Accessed December 29, 2020. https://www.cdc.gov/nchs/products/databriefs/db377.htm#section_4.

[11] Roth, David L., William E. Haley, Martha Hovater, Martinique Perkins, Virginia G. Wadley, Suzanne Judd. 2013. "Family Caregiving and All-Cause Mortality: Findings from a Population-based Propensity-matched Analysis." *American Journal of Epidemiology*, Volume 178, Issue 10, 15 November 2013, Pages 1571–1578, https://doi.org/10.1093/aje/kwt225

## Chapter 1

[12] Individuals with Disabilities Education Act. n.d. https://sites.ed.gov/idea/.

# Chapter 2

[13] Williamson, Marcus. 2017. *"Jon Underwood, Founder of Death Café."* The Independent, July 21, 2017. https://www.independent.co.uk/news/obituaries/jon-underwood-founder-death-cafe-a7850331.html

[14] National Institute on Aging, U.S. Department of Health & Human Services. n.d. Advanced Care Planning: Healthcare Directives https://www.nia.nih.gov/health/advance-care-planning-healthcare-directives

[15] Medicare.gov. n.d. Advanced directives & long-term care. https://www.medicare.gov/manage-your-health/advance-directives-long-term-care

[16] National POLST. n.d. National POLST Form: Portable Medical Order. https://polst.org/national-form/?-pro=1

[17] Five Wishes. n.d. https://fivewishes.org/

[18] Ibid

# Chapter 3

[19] Dweck, Carol S. 2006. *Mindset: The New Psychology of Success*. New York: Random House.

[20] Ibid.

# Chapter 4

[21] Rosenberg, Matt. 2020. "Generational Names in the United States: Traditionalist, Gen Zs, and Everything in Between." Thoughtco.com. https://www.thoughtco.com/names-of-generations-1435472

[22] Behavioral Gerontology. 2019. Fact Sheet https://www.bacb.com/wp-content/uploads/2020/05/Behavioral-Gerontology-Fact-Sheet_190520.pdf. Accessed May 2019.

[23] Applied Behavior Analysis Edu.com. n.d. What is Behavioral Gerontology? https://www.appliedbehavioranalysisedu.org/behavioral-gerontology/. Accessed December 29, 2020.

[24] Rotolo, Candace. 2020. UTIs Cause Unusual Behavioral Symptoms in Elders. AgingCare.com. https://www.agingcare.com/articles/urinary-tract-infection-symptoms-151547.htm.

# Chapter 5

[25] Ibid.

[26] Commission for case management certification. https://ccmcertification.org/about-ccmc/about-case-management/definition-and-philosophy-case-management accessed February 26, 2021.

# Chapter 6

[27] MindTools.com. SMART Goals https://www.mindtools.com/pages/article/smart-goals.htm. Accessed January 12, 2020.

[28] Anxiety and Depression Association of America. n.d. Exercise for Stress and Anxiety. https://adaa.org/living-with-anxiety/managing-anxiety/exercise-stress-and-anxiety. Accessed December 29, 2020.

[29] SleepFoundation.org. n.d. How to Reset Your Sleep Routine. https://www.sleepfoundation.org/sleep-hygiene/how-to-reset-your-sleep-routine. Accessed April 10, 2020.

[30] Kramer, Jillian. 2019. "7 Foods That Secretly Stress You Out." EatingWell.com. January 2019 http://www.eatingwell.com/article/291444/7-foods-that-secretly-stress-you-out/.

[31] TheWaterWay.com. 2020. "Can Staying Hydrated Reduce Anxiety?" April 2, 2020 https://thewaterway.com/can-staying-hydrated-reduce-anxiety/.

[32] ClevelandClinic.org. 2019. "For Stress Relief, Research Says: 'Hug it Out.'" January 18, 2019. https://newsroom.clevelandclinic.org/2019/01/18/for-stress-relief-research-says-hug-it-out/

[33] Laskowski, Edward, R. Mayo Clinic. 1998-2020. "How much should the average adult exercise every day?" Mayo Foundation for Medical Education and Research (MFMER). https://www.mayoclinic.org/healthy-lifestyle/fitness/expert-answers/exercise/faq-20057916#:~:text=Get%20at%20least%20150%20minutes,provide%20even%20greater%20health%20benefit. Accessed April 10, 2020.

[34] Greaves, Kayla. 2019. "How Your Skin and Skincare Routine Can Impact Your Mental Health." Instyle.com. December 20, 2019. https://www.instyle.com/beauty/skin-conditions-skincare-mental-health.

[35] Markowitz, Fred E. "Involvement in Mental Health Self-Help Groups and Recovery." Health sociology review: The Journal of the Health Section of the Australian Sociological Association vol. 24,2 (2015): 199-212. doi:10.1080/14461242.2015.1015149

[36] Heid, Markham. 2018. "You Asked: Is It Bad for You to Read the News Constantly?" Time.com. https://time.com/5125894/is-reading-news-bad-for-you/.

[37] Burnett-Zeigler, Inger et al. 2016. "Mind-Body Approaches to Treating Mental Health Symptoms Among Disadvantaged Populations: A Comprehensive Review." Journal of Alternative and Complementary Medicine (New York, N.Y.) vol. 22,2 (2016): 115-24. doi:10.1089/acm.2015.0038 Accessed December 2018.

[38] Stapleton, Peta. 2019. The Science Behind Tapping: A Proven Stress Management Technique for the Mind & Body. Hay House, Inc.

[39] Chong, Cecilia, S.M., Megumi Tsunaka, Hector Tsang, Edard Chang, and Wai Mind Cheung. 2011. "Effects of Yoga on Stress Management in Healthy Adults: A Systematic Review." Alternative Therapies in Health and Medicine. Aliso Viejo. Vol. 17, Issue 1 (Jan/Feb): 32-8.

[40] Sauer, Mary. 2018. Medically reviewed by Daniel Bubnis, M.S., NASM-CPT, NASE Level II-CSS. https://www.healthline.com/health/tai-chi-benefits. Accessed March 1, 2020.

[41] Healthbeat. 2011. "Giving thanks can make you happier." Harvard Health Publishing, Harvard Medical School. https://www.health.harvard.edu/healthbeat/giving-thanks-can-make-you-happier. Accessed April 10, 2020.

[42] Mayo Clinic. 1998-2020. Menopause. Mayo Foundation for Medical Education and Research (MFMER). https://www.mayoclinic.org/diseases-conditions/menopause/symptoms-causes/syc-20353397#:~:text=Menopause%20is%20the%20time%20that,is%20a%20natural%20biological%20process. Accessed December 29, 2020.

# Chapter 7

[43] Elwert, Felix, and Nicholas A. Christakis. "The effect of widowhood on mortality by the causes of death of both spouses." *American Journal of Public Health* vol. 98,11 (2008): 2092-8. doi:10.2105/AJPH.2007.114348. Accessed December 29. 2020.

# Chapter 8

[44] Ibid.

[45] Zagorsky, Jay, L. 2013. Do People Save or Spend Their Inheritances? Understanding What happens to Inherited Wealth. Journal of Family and Economic Issues 34, 64-76.

[46] The Money Mender https://themoneymender.com/. Accessed April 10, 2019.

[47] LGBTQ https://www.nolo.com/legal-encyclopedia/six-key-estate-planning-issues-gay-lesbian-couples.html. Accessed April 10, 2019.

[48] HIPAA https://www.hhs.gov/hipaa/index.html. Accessed December 29, 2020.

[49] The Balance https://www.thebalance.com/. Accessed December 29, 2020.

# Chapter 9

[50] Burrell, Alexander, and Lucy E. Selman. 2020. "How do Funeral Practices Impact Bereaved Relatives' Mental Health, Grief and Bereavement? A Mixed Methods Review with Implications for COVID-19." *Omega – Journal of Death and Dying: Sage Journals.* Published online. https://journals.sagepub.com/doi/full/10.1177/0030222820941296; Huibertha B. Mitima-Verloop, Trudy T. M. Mooren, and Paul A. Boelen (2019) "Facilitating Grief: An Exploration of the Function of Funerals and Rituals in Relation to Grief Reactions." Death Studies. DOI: 10.1080/07481187.2019.1686090.

# Chapter 10

[51] Kübler-Ross, Elisabeth. *1993 On Death and Dying*

[52] Kessler, David. 2019. *Finding Meaning: The Sixth Stage of Grief.* New York: Simon & Schuster.

[53] Grief.com https://grief.com/misconceptions/

Made in the USA
Las Vegas, NV
08 March 2022

45270180R00095